The Emerging Worldwide
Electronic University

Recent Titles in
Contributions to the Study of Education

The Emerging Worldwide Electronic University

INFORMATION AGE GLOBAL HIGHER EDUCATION

Parker Rossman

PRAEGER STUDIES ON THE 21st CENTURY

PRAEGER

Westport, Connecticut
London

The Library of Congress has cataloged the Greenwood
Press edition as follows:

Rossman, Parker.
    The emerging worldwide electronic university : information age
global higher education / Parker Rossman.
        p.   cm. – (Contributions to the study of education, ISSN
0196-707X ; no. 57)
    Includes bibliographical references (p.) and index.
    ISBN 0-313-27927-6 (alk. paper)
    1. International education.   2. Distance education.   I. Title.
II. Series.
LC1090.R65   1992
378.1'7078 – dc20   92-3660

British Library Cataloguing in Publication Data is available.

A hardcover edition of *The Emerging Worldwide Electronic University* is available
from the Greenwood Press imprint of Greenwood Publishing Group, Inc.
(Contributions to the Study of Education, Number 57; ISBN: 0-313-27927-6).

Library of Congress Catalog Card Number: 92-3660
ISBN: 0-275-94776-9
ISSN: 1070-1850

First published in 1993

Praeger Publishers, 88 Post Road West, Westport, CT 06881
An imprint of Greenwood Publishing Group, Inc.

Printed in the United States of America

∞™

The paper used in this book complies with the
Permanent Paper Standard issued by the National
Information Standards Organization (Z39.48-1984).

10 9 8 7 6 5 4 3 2

CONTENTS

Acknowledgments

The nature and the future of the university have been subjects of much of my research life, and I owe these interests mostly to Sir Walter Moberly and a study group of British graduate students of various disciplines who concluded that the first obligation of the scholar is to help the university be true to its highest calling.

I owe credit to all of the people cited as references, but especially to H.J.A. Goodman of the University of Calgary; James Grier Miller and Joseph Becker of the University of the World; Takeshi Utsumi of GLO-SAS/Global University project; Richard Kirby, administrator of Mensa; Donald Straus, former president of the American Arbitration Association and other members of the Columbia University faculty seminar "Computers, Man, and Society," where sections of this book have been discussed. Others who read parts of this manuscript or who have provided me with unpublished papers and reports include Charles Urbanowicz, anthropologist at California State University at Chico; Roy Lundin, Australian distance education specialist; the late Robert Smith of NASA; Robert Bonn, sociologist at City University of New York (CUNY) and secretary of the GLOSAS/Global University project; Steven Rosen also of CUNY; Glynn Harmon of the Graduate School of Library and Information Science at the University of Texas; President Lionel Baldwin of the National Technological University; Joseph Pelton, formerly of INTELSAT and now director of the University of Colorado's Interdisciplinary Telecommunications Program; David Hughes, consultant on Big Sky connections to Japan; Paul Levinson of ConnectEd; Martin Chamberlain of the University of the World; Gregory Wright of *New Sense* newsletter; Michael Moore, director of the Center for the Study of Distance Education; Jerome Glenn of United Nations University; John Bollier of Yale; Charles Ess of Drury College; June Andel and other members of the ASIS World Brain group; Vincent Darago of the Foundation for International Broadcasting; Stan Pokras of the Public Interest Media Project; and John Steward of the Commonwealth of Learning.

Although my bibliography mostly lists printed materials, I must not understate the help received from on-line journals and computer conferences—for example: DEOS of the Center for the Study of Distance Education; GLOSAS-L from the University of Ottawa; *Netweaver* on-line journal; the EIES conference on computer technology for developing nations, and others which have opened many doors to experts, consultants, researchers, and overseas educators.

Also, credit must be given to organizations as well as individuals since so much of what is happening is emerging through collective processes. Some examples follow.

The annual meetings of the board of the University of the World have enabled me to get information from distance education pioneers from many countries including China and the Soviet Union—for example: Lord Perry of Walton, pioneer at the British Open University; Peter Meincke, former president of the University of Prince Edward Island; Dr. Gabriel Betancur, former Associate General Secretary of UNESCO; Rodrigo Carazo, former president of Costa Rica; United Nations consultant Rashmi Mayur, chair of the India Council of the University of the World; Dr. Kjell Samuelson of the University of Stockholm, pioneer in offering degree programs from one country to another.

At conferences of the World Future Society I have helped conduct demonstrations of the "global classroom" and have presented sections of this book at workshops. The WFS's education conferences, especially, have been occasions for meeting pioneering educational researchers and for demonstrations involving people like Robert Muller, former Associate General Secretary of the United Nations, and, in 1991, president of the United Nations University in Costa Rica.

The Electronic Networking Association and its members such as Nelson Heller (*The Heller Report*) and Dwight Steward have been especially helpful. Steward invited me to present a section of this book there.

The American Association for Information Science where I have been invited to speak on topics from this book has provided an occasion to get ideas from a fascinating range of people.

And finally my contact with the officers, conferences, and global technology demonstrations of GLOSAS (Global Systems Analysis and Simulation) and its Global University project, especially President Takeshi Utsumi and all of the university people in East Asia and Latin America with whom GLOSAS has been working to deregulate barriers to extending electronic connections for education, has been most important and valuable.

I am also grateful to those who have responded to some of the material in this book in *The Futurist, Breakthrough* of Global Education Associates, the *American Journal of Distance Education, T.H.E. Journal, Transpersonal Perspectives* in Switzerland, *World Visions,* and other publications.

Special appreciation is also due to editorial consultant Ben Boyinton; to my editors at Greenwood; to my wife; to my brother, Vern; and to librarians at Yale University and at the East Lyme public library (where the unseen librarians work such marvels through interlibrary loan and electronic data base searches). The term *emerging* in the title seems justified by the increasing volume of new information which, too late for inclusion in this volume, continues to appear each month.

Introduction: Fish Imagining Fire

> As the artificial walls of our great universities come tumbling down through technology, and as electronic networks expand the reach of university campuses, the range of influence of higher education will increase. . . . The teaching of the best professors . . . will be available . . . to anyone who wants to learn.
>
> John Sculley, 1988

John Sculley (president of Apple Computers) predicts that "the universities as networks of interdependence" are going to be at the center of a new renaissance. Most educators are more modest in their expectations, yet just as banking, entertainment, and politics are being transformed by global telecommunications, something remarkable may also be happening in higher education. It may be two decades before we can be sure.

Meanwhile, this book proposes an agenda—questions, not answers—for those who plan for and seek to give some direction to the expanding use of computer conferencing and television for international courses. Such developments are multiplying so rapidly that it is difficult to keep up with them.

Our title includes four suggestive words. The first is *emerging*. We cannot as yet be sure what is happening or how important it is going to be. Some scholars see a change in all human institutions more fundamental than anything humanity has experienced in five thousand years. (For example, see Sutton 1990; Singhal and Rogers 1989.) The important thing: now is the time to begin planning for twenty years ahead.

The second word is *electronic*, the technology (satellite, optic cable, microchip, etc.) that makes possible the cooperative exchange of lectures and courses on a global basis, including the virtual global-scale lecture hall. It is, however, a mistake to begin with the technology. Educators need to decide how higher education can and should be restructured to meet the needs of six billion people in an increasingly global society and then develop the technology that best serves these ends:

- adequate food for all the world's people
- adequate health care, housing, and economic opportunity for all
- restoration of the ecology of the planet, reduced pollution of air, soil, and water
- justice for all through global governance adequate to solve conflicts without war
- accomplishment of the goals stated in the United Nations Declaration on Human Rights
- economic opportunity for all
- education for all, to make possible the other goals

More important than the technology is "expanding global community" (Naisbitt and Aburdene 1990). Technology that can put more power in the hands of people can be developed and used to enable and to further such goals—based on right combinations of cost effectiveness as well as earnability—rather than merely using technology developed by non-educators or by commercial interests (see Pelton 1989; Jussawalla, Okuma, and Araki 1989; Gilder 1990).

The third is *university*, a word that includes "universe." Higher education is a crucial foundation for the emerging information-and-knowledge-based society. Historically, the end of the twentieth century is a time comparable to the twelfth century when the rise of the university in western Europe helped enable the Renaissance. The word university first referred to a guild of students, then to a guild of scholars. From the beginning the universities were international. Students often traveled in search of the course they wanted, wandering from country to country much as some now explore the "electronic highways."

The original universities had very little organization, although there was a vigorous intellectual life. At Paris, for example, the university "was not founded, it grew" (Haskins 1927). Its first charter simply recognized a body of students and teachers that already existed. Similarly today, no international government agency is establishing a new global system of higher education. Yet the electronic university seems to be emerging and is closely related to concerns of leading educators. (For example, see Bok 1990; Smith 1990; Becker 1989; Merriam and Cunningham 1989.)

Roy Lundin (1988) reports that tens of millions of people are participating in distance education, open universities, and other electronic learning networks. As such programs expand globally, sharing of information and courses can be a much more affordable form of aid to the Third World (see Krueger and Ruttan 1989). Ivan Trujillo, administrator of the Universidad de Los Andes in Bogota, Colombia, has pointed out that inflation and interest on huge foreign debts are having profound impacts upon education in Latin America (Trujillo 1988). Whereas in the 1960s it was still possible to send large numbers of gifted Latin American students abroad for graduate studies, it is now prohibitively expensive to do so. At the same time a "dangerous information gap" is causing developing nations to fall far behind. Scholars in Latin America and their universities often cannot even afford the increasingly expensive scholarly journals that are essential if they are to keep up with current developments in their own fields of research. So perhaps the best solution is to enlarge electronic connections from Latin America to the major university systems of the world.

Also, Trujillo says, Latin Americans confront an already stale idea of what universities should be. They too often see them as almost a luxury, a place to educate a professional elite. Moving to change this, Trujillo's university was the first in South America to join the North American university computer consortium, EDUCOM. As the universities of East Asia, North America, and Europe expand their electronic connections, he said, Latin Americans also "want in."

Worldwide, however, is the key word. Higher education has been slow in coming to terms with the emerging global society, and many educators do not yet seem to be concerned that the shape of the electronic university may be determined or straitjacketed by global noneducation forces such as business, technological developments, and other government priorities. It is therefore crucial that attention now be given to discussion and development of the goals, priorities, values, and philosophy that ought to govern global higher education. It is hoped that a great deal of academic freedom can be maintained in the balance between government, academia, volunteer, and private educational organizations, and the business corporations involved in continuing education, so that no one of these commercial or bureaucratic forces will dominate. (For example, see Schiller 1989.) This requires replacing cumbersome, bureaucratic institutions with flexible networks in which scholars can link themselves together on a global basis.

This book is the first comprehensive effort to gather together and summarize scattered research reports and to report experiments and demonstrations that suggest that a worldwide electronic university is emerging. The publisher's space limitations require that I merely cite many of the reports, case studies, and the chapters that introduced the tentative proposals of some long-range planning committees. Also I have left out detailed descriptions of technology, although some definitions remain in the text (see index).

It is difficult to write both for educators who have been too busy to keep up with these developments and also for those who are experts in one phase or another of what is reported here. It is even harder to write both for educators in the developed nations and for those in less privileged countries—where many are eager to find out whether or not the electronic sharing of courses can help solve some of their problems.

I write this in the first person as a reminder that I alone am responsible for the incompleteness, errors, and other faults in what is the fruit of a six-year exploration of a vast literature and of attending conferences and studying reports. Pulling it all together has been an exhausting task and at times a nearly impossible one. This compilation should be seen as a precursor of a more adequate book to come, one which will also require the collaboration of many researchers and experimenters in global higher education. I am grateful for those in many countries (most of them cited in the bibliography) who have helped me gather this information because they feel that the time has come for this kind of introduction and survey.

New possibilities for global electronic higher education are also often raised in conferences that were not intended to be about education— for example, the June 26–27, 1991, conference of Computer Professionals for Social Responsibility (Cisler 1991). My focus here, however, is on organizations that offer or plan to offer courses from one country to another, or those that are asking questions about standards, offering degrees, types of administration and funding, and about ethics and values. For example, how can sharing between the First and Third Worlds be best accomplished without colonialist interference? What philosophical principles should underlie global higher education?

As we confront the possibilities of the technology, we are, to use a phrase of Arthur C. Clarke's, like fish trying to imagine fire. If some new kind of global higher education institution is coming into existence, however, it is propelled not only by the new opportunities provided by communications technology, but also by the desperate needs of underdeveloped areas for better research, political action, and education.

The Emerging Worldwide
Electronic University

One

Signs of the Emerging Space Age University

It is fair to say that the network is becoming the favorite structure
in the way we arrange our lives.

Jay Bolter 1991

Many higher education institutions are experimenting with the exchange
of courses and lectures from country to country, and some are asking
how else universities in poorer countries can keep pace with scientific
research that is crucial to their future. Millions of students take courses
electronically, many scholars use electronic networks for global-scale
research projects, and other signs point to the emergence of a worldwide
electronic university. Planning groups are asking if a messy "kludge"
is inevitable or if all those involved in distance and electronic education,
including business corporations, can be brought into some more comprehensive joint planning.

Robert Mueller, who brought imaginative leadership to the United
Nations, and who is now head of the United Nations University of Peace
in Costa Rica, says that he would like to devote some of his retirement
to imagining what the ideal university should be like. Is the ideal university to be a high-tech research institution in one location, such as the
proposed Japanese-Australian joint project to be located near Adelaide
but with electronic involvements all over the world?

Or is the university of the future already coming into existence in hyperspace (where two people meet during a long-distance phone call or meet on interactive TV or on a computer network)? Or in cyberspace (computer-created environments)?

Many people first encountered the exchange of courses from one country to another by interactive television when they read in 1988 newspapers that Tufts University in Boston and Moscow State University were offering a joint course. Students at both universities heard the same lectures, were assigned the same readings, and engaged in joint class discussions via global television (Chrepta 1988).

In September 1988, President Jean Mayer of Tufts University chaired a conference at Talloires in France of forty-five university presidents from all over the world, an almost unprecedented meeting of educators from "all regions and many cultures" (Van Kamp 1988). The participants drafted a declaration, a call to all the sixty million students and two million researchers involved in higher education throughout the world. In a world "that is plagued by war, hunger, injustice and suffering," the educators endorsed the exchange of information by communications based on relatively low-cost technologies that, they said, can provide access to computer networks and afford two-way television linkage among university classrooms in various parts of the world, thereby creating a truly "global classroom."

This, they said, can enable research and teaching programs to increase a common understanding of the cause of conflicts and their resolution, the relationship between peace and development, and the sources of injustice and hunger. Thus the universities can "better discharge our responsibilities to educate men and women who will lead our societies in the twenty-first century."

Affirming that differences in regional perspectives and academic traditions will necessarily create a diversity in teaching and research, they aspired to more "commonality" (their term) in their educational programs. They agreed that universities should make every effort to support regional academic associations and in other ways encourage the development of "regional centers" to assist in the organization of research, the exchange of information and curricula, and the development of faculty. Can reasonably priced—yet global-scale—communications and computer-empowered learning tools now thus make possible for all people the kinds of learning and research which the space age requires?

A WORLDWIDE ELECTRONIC UNIVERSITY?

We see signs of an international electronic university even before all of its institutional forms exist:

1. Students in one country are taking courses in another via computer conference and/or television or using combinations of other technologies (see chapter 4).

2. Catalogs of courses from many universities and countries are available electronically to prospective students in other countries (see chapter 10).

3. An international faculty at first perhaps simply consists of all teachers who offer courses electronically and all researchers who collaborate electronically with colleagues in other countries (see chapter 5).

4. University administration or governance involves networks of those in colleges, universities, government agencies, professional associations, and business corporations who are assigned to plan and administer such electronic education programs (see chapter 2).

5. Electronic classrooms and other facilities exist where students and faculty meet in "hyperspace" (see chapter 8).

6. Student activities, coffee houses, clubs, and action projects begin to involve students electronically from and to more than one country (see chapter 8).

7. Provision for guidance and counseling. (A student in Singapore meets with his advisor in British Columbia whenever she wishes on a computer network.)

8. An emerging global electronic university library (see chapter 6).

9. "Co-laboratory" facilities, through which scientists undertake lab work together, connect them electronically across national boundaries (see chapter 5).

10. Special event lectures and student action/convocations (such as global "live aid" concerts) are shared from country to country.

11. On-line electronic bookstores are available for students in another country to use in ordering print books or downloading electronic ones.

12. Faculty meetings and faculty training can be shared from country to country electronically.

13. Many scholars, without leaving home, participate electronically in international conferences of associations of scholars who meet by discipline and profession. A few international scholarly and scientific journals begin to appear on-line, computer cross-indexed for instant search and retrieval.

14. Continuing education conferences and workshops exist (as in the National University Teleconferencing Network) in which participants from more than one country participate electronically.

15. Electronic bulletin boards exist on the hyperspace campus.

16. And a worldwide electronic university press? "It is time to talk about joining institutions in a vast and powerful system for scholarly communication," says the director of the New York State Library. A uni-

versity-based publishing network to "bring order to the . . . inexorably growing online publication process" is beginning (Yavarkovsky 1990).

In addition to the above list of university programs and functions, the term "emerging world university" suggests that much of what is going on is not yet "seen" by many people in higher education and also that in a sense this emerging international electronic university consists of all electronic cooperation and exchange among students, faculty, and researchers.

THE DREAM OF A WORLD UNIVERSITY

Following the second world war, there were hundreds of proposals for world universities or other new forms of international higher education for intellectual enquiry and exchange among scholars of all countries and all fields of knowledge.

A 1988 conference in Campinas, Brazil, was called by the heads of eleven Latin American and seven European countries. They met to follow up on an idea (developed in 1983 at a conference of the International Association of Universities) about how to help colleges with low academic standards. The only way for developing countries to keep up, one participant said, "is the creation of a global university system in which all higher education institutions share their resources."

Robert Bonn of the City University of New York, secretary of the GLOSAS/Global University project, asks about the values embodied in higher education. Is the driving force of the emerging space-age university simply a further development of existing international course exchange and cooperation among scholars? *Or* a dissemination of specialized western knowledge to the masses? *Or* some kind of empowerment of local people to develop their own technologies/approaches to environmental/social problems? He asks about values such as sharing educational resources with more people, lower cost for the earth's poor, orientation to democracy, focus on peace, and the creation of new educational communities. Others have asked how "every peasant" can get more adequate education in agriculture, medical treatment, sanitation, and community organization. There were dreams—but no idea how to fulfill them—for teachers in all countries to enrich each other's experience; for Peace Corps young people in many countries to meet and share experiences; and for enlarging the vision and skills of political leaders. Others proposed joint scientific enterprises and research, aided by television, and cited the International Oceanographic project and the International Geophysical Year to show what can be done through cooperative effort on the part of the world's scholars and scientists. The next step, however, would be to reach all the world's students, and how could this be done?

BEGINNINGS OF DISTANCE EDUCATION

Some universities have been negotiating with similar schools in other countries to offer joint courses electronically: for example, Dartmouth College to offer a joint course in Business Administration with International University in Tokyo and City University of New York to cooperate with Fudan University in China. An expansion of the globalization of education can also be seen in the overseas branches of many universities, such as the joint American-Japanese colleges that have been developing under Japanese funding and initiative, and in such proposals as that of President Jimmy Carter at the 1990 EDUCOM conference. He repeated his plea for more universities in the industrial countries to adopt and share resources with less privileged universities in other nations.

The Corporation for Public Broadcasting reported as early as 1987 that 50 percent of American colleges were using telecourses to present instruction to off-campus students. As such electronic course sharing and projects continue to expand to other continents, they multiply to the extent to which it is almost impossible to keep track of them.

Some overseas course offerings are from government agencies such as the United States Air Force Extension Institute. Others, for example, to sailors on ships, are from commercial operations such as the American Open University.

Many students in other countries now take courses electronically from universities in Europe, Canada, and the United States. To cite two examples among many: students in places as distant and divergent as Russia, Yugoslavia, Singapore, and Venezuela take courses via computer conference from the ConnectEd program at the New School for Social Research in New York; and the University of British Columbia has offered social science courses to students in Asia.

The electronic exchange of lectures and courses builds upon the long experience of colleges with "distance education" programs offered via radio, television, and more recently via computer conference. Through its Project Share, for example, INTELSAT (the international satellite agency) has enabled the Chinese TV university to reach a million students with 5,000 receive-only antennae via three transponders (Pelton 1990).

An anthropologist and a media specialist (Nevins and Urbanowicz 1991) have reported American West Coast beginnings of what they call "extra-terrestrial education" (via satellite). Although they warn of the dangers of simplification in such a complex area, what they report is summarized here and is suggestive of the order and timetable for similar developments elsewhere in the world:

- In a sense, the history begins with correspondence courses offered by mail, expanding often from one country to another during the last century.
- Radio broadcast of college courses existed in Iowa as early as 1933 and "open universities" in many countries now provide college courses to millions of students via radio and television.
- Advanced Instructional TV was used in California in 1969 when courses at Stanford University were offered to professionals at their work places when it was difficult for them to come to the Stanford campus. By 1975, California State University, Chico, had developed an instructional system to offer courses via TV across the northern part of the state.
- Satellites then made international courses possible. In 1981, for example, the Hewlett Packard Corporation "began constructing a satellite network, designed to link Palo Alto with more than a hundred downlink sites around North America" (Nevins and Urbanowicz 1991).
- In 1982, the National University Teleconferencing Network (NUTN) was created, with headquarters at Oklahoma State University, to offer "a wide variety of programs by satellite."
- In 1984, the California State University, Chico, began to offer courses electronically to off-campus students, that could lead to an M.S. degree in computer science.
- Also in 1984, the National Technological University (NTU), a consortium of university departments of engineering, began to offer courses and then graduate degrees to engineers whose work made it difficult for them to come to campus, or who needed to update their skills on-site. By 1989, the NTU was exploring the possibility of offering its courses to students in East Asia.
- By 1990, fifty-four electronic networks were involved in educational programming via satellite throughout North America, including schools, colleges, business corporations, and professional groups. Instruction was offered in medicine, law, banking, insurance, law enforcement, auto repairs, and much more.
- Interactive electronic teaching programs had meanwhile also come into existence in other countries. Students in Scandinavia, for example, were taking doctoral studies with courses from more than one country with hardly a visit to the campus that awarded the degree.

WHY SUCH ELECTRONIC PROGRAMS?

In places like Alaska, Australia, and Montana, where many primary and secondary school students are scattered in remote areas, youngsters have for a long time been taught at home via radio (packet-type radio can now be used to connect computers) and television. Increasingly now, scattered, snowbound, or ill pupils can be directly involved in a classroom, participating as if actually there. In this same way education can be offered to the world, and later also to people who spend extended periods of time on space stations.

At present, the leaders of higher education tend to think that such electronic programs can only supplement traditional kinds of on-campus education and expand distance education and "extension courses." But smaller colleges can greatly enlarge and enrich their offerings by drawing upon such electronic resources; after all, no university can offer everything! (See Graham 1991.)

As soon as the human community gets the will to do so, it will be possible for educators to extend to the world the opportunity that a rural county in New York State (Pelton 1990) and some other American states are now seeking to offer to every high school student. If, in a remote rural high school, there are one or two pupils who want to take some course that their small school is unable to offer, such as calculus or Chinese, those students can be connected to a college or another high school where such a course is offered. Without leaving their own schools, such students can connect to a distant class on an Indian reservation via interactive cable TV or two telephone lines, one for listening and talking and the other for two-way viewing by television screen.

Many such technologies are increasingly available so that the distance students, sitting at their computer monitors, can participate just as if they were in the classroom and it allows instructors to see and correct what distant students are writing. Research shows that, when tested, and even when in prison, such distance students are doing as well as— and sometimes even better than—the students who are actually sitting in the classroom (Grimes, Nielson, Niss 1989). This is true even when a Pennsylvania student is connected to a classroom in Utah or Hawaii. And it can be equally true for a student connected to a class in Germany or Japan as demonstrated by teachers at the University of Hawaii who showed what can come into foreign language study when students in America and Japan meet electronically as if they were in the same classroom, conversing together in each other's language.

So one sees the beginnings of a country to country sharing of resources that can enrich and bring enhanced quality into any school in the world, whether in distant jungle or isolated desert.

DEATH OF THE UNIVERSITY AS WE HAVE KNOWN IT?

A New York University dean, Herbert L. London (1987), has predicted the end of the university as most Americans picture it—four happy years on a resident campus. Half of American students in 1990 were older than the traditional college age. Many people complete their college educations or take graduate degrees on a part-time basis as commuters, taking courses across many working years. Many corporations now operate extensive college-level training programs for their employees overseas, wherever they are; IBM, for example, is said to operate the largest "university" in the world and several such corporations have joined forces with universities in Europe to create EuroPace and the PALIO project that offer courses electronically to their employees.

Unless universities can agree upon plans to guide and coordinate these electronic developments, the largest share of higher education in the world may indeed fall into the hands of business corporations or for-profit educational institutions.

When the New York University dean spoke of the "death of the university," however, he also had in mind the numbers of college faculty around the world not now engaged in serious research. Humanity is entering a period of history in which we are confronted with overwhelming problems that require more serious work that must engage teams of scholars who are often scattered around the globe (see chapter 5).

The dean also reported an "education malaise" in which universities are failing to prepare students for the sort of world we have, much less for the space/information age in which they will live in the next century. In a time of rapid change and accelerated growth of knowledge, people need lifetime connections to higher education. Electronic courses can be sent to people wherever they are, whenever they have need for it, and can be pursued part-time and at any hour of day or night. Many traditional universities are in fact changing rapidly to serve a globally interdependent society that requires much more than mere dissemination of facts.

BEYOND TRADITIONAL DISTANCE EDUCATION

It is not easy to define distance education (Keegan 1989; Garrison and Shale 1989). The problem is to find a middle ground between the ideal and the existing reality. New electronic technologies have blurred the boundaries between on-campus and distance education. Definition is complicated by the almost infinite variety of electronic programs and possibilities. For example, Desmond Keegan's early "descriptive definition" noted that distance education learners are usually taught as individuals and not in groups. Yet today the electronic connection may be class to class or college to college, not only to individual students.

Conventional theorists, Keegan continued, have tended to say that a student either attends a class in person or studies at a distance. Yet, in fact, half of the members of a class may be at a distant location or a resident student's courses may be partly on campus and partly electronic from off campus. Electronic programs can enrich the educational possibilities of learners both at a distance and on campus. However, at present and perhaps for some time, electronic education programs will likely be primarily for people who cannot come in person to attend courses on a campus or will primarily interest college faculty and graduate students who need access to up-to-date information in their research specialty.

A number of distance education programs and organizations have taken initiatives that are leading to the development of the emerging electronic university. One, for example, is the International Center for Distance Learning (ICDL), a documentation center located at the British Open University's Institute of Educational Technology (see Paulsen 1991). This center has been particularly helpful in the establishment of the "Commonwealth of Learning (COL)," described in the next chapter, which brings together the "open universities" within what used to be called the British Commonwealth.

The ICDL is unique in that it is established to be a research center on distance and international electronic education. Its integrated computerized data base is accessible from America and includes a beginning catalog of information on universities offering courses electronically, subjects taught, media used, entrance requirements, and information on specific courses available from Commonwealth institutions. Administrators, government officials, and researchers visiting the ICDL include planners responsible for creating new distance-teaching institutions or for introducing distance teaching into existing institutions and organizations.

NOT JUST ACADEMIC INSTITUTIONS

It now seems that the shape of global higher education is not going to be determined by government and universities alone, since international business corporations are already major partners in the enterprise. As Peter Drucker (1989) has pointed out, continuing education of the already highly schooled, as well as of employees who need new skills, has become so important that "the business enterprise is increasingly going to be an educational institution."

OFFICIAL U.S. GOVERNMENTAL
ELECTRONIC EDUCATION

Perhaps the program in the United States that comes closest to being the COL sort of open university would be the 1.3 million students who, by 1989, had taken courses via the Public Broadcasting System (PBS-

TV). The PBS Adult Learning Service was by 1990 in partnership with 1,500 colleges and local PBS-TV stations (Brock 1990). It offers courses in science, math, humanities, government, psychology, business, and history. Training courses offered through one of the four PBS educational channels are available at work sites and colleges as well as at home, and are on satellite accessible from some other nations.

Some of the programs are free; some of the programs are funded by tuition paid by students and by license fees paid by colleges or business corporations that use the courses. In 1991 PBS was preparing to offer much more educational programming within satellite limitations via "compressed signals." Five to ten days of courses can be transmitted within a limited time (twenty at once when Telstar is launched in 1993) so that TV stations can offer them later when they want to.

The U. S. armed forces have cooperated with educational institutions to make it possible for some overseas personnel to take courses via "the electronic university." During their months in the Persian Gulf in 1990–91 many American sailors took such courses (Turner 1990b) through the Annenberg Corporation for Public Broadcasting System project. With various combinations of technology, it was reported that over 4,000 enlisted U. S. Navy personnel on some seventy ships had enrolled in telecourses, with 80 percent of them completing the courses for college credit. The American Open University program of the New York School of Technology has for several years been offering credit courses to sailors on ships.

COURSES OFFERED ON COMMERCIAL COMPUTER NETWORKS

Theoretically, the courses that have been offered by the Electronic University Network (EUN) on the CompuServe commercial computer network have been available to students overseas. "Founded in 1983 by TeleLearning, Inc., the EUN has helped thousands of students earn college degrees and credits in their own homes" (Elias 1987). Credit toward a degree is possible for EUN students either through a cooperating college or through standardized tests such as the College Level Examination Program. In any case, the degree has actually been offered by one of the higher education institutions (such as the New York Regents College) that have cooperated with EUN. The CompuServe network itself has seen the EUN as "a new educational delivery system [that] provides a new kind of interaction between instructor and class, even though classmates may be thousands of miles apart" (Elias 1987).

David Hughes (1991) is convinced that he was the first to offer a credit course on-line. This was in 1981 on the (commercial) Source computer network. Now, he says, courses on commercial networks such as

CompuServe or TWICS in Japan are available to anyone in the world who has a telephone and modem.

Although still a rather small program when judged by the number of courses offered overseas and the number of overseas students involved, the ConnectEd program of the New School for Social Research in New York City also deserves special mention as a demonstration of a major alternative to TV courses. This program worked in close cooperation with the EIES computer network of New Jersey Institute of Technology, which has made courses available to students in many countries.

The ConnectEd program has, for example, offered Master's programs in media studies, including legal and philosophical questions; in electronic publishing; on science fiction and myth in the space age; and a seminar on McLuhan. Its courses, and a very able faculty willing to experiment with distance education via computer network, have attracted overseas students also interested in such experimentation. (See Levinson 1991 and chapter 10.)

CABLE TELEVISION COURSES

Credit courses available on U.S. cable television are already available to some other countries via satellite. Domestically in the United States, the Mind Extension University (MEU), for example, delivers educational programming to homes and businesses via cable TV. The MEU offers MBA degree and college credit courses through eleven major institutions of higher education. MEU is a subsidiary of Jones International, Ltd., a global communications corporation and the world's largest cable TV management system. The company's literature affirms a commitment to "the extension of the human mind" by using cable TV, telecommunications and satellite to deliver "for credit" and "noncredit" continuing educational opportunities. The MEU curriculum has included the innovative telecourses funded by the Annenberg Corporation for Public Broadcasting as well as those produced by institutions such as Miami-Dade Community College. There have been no restrictions on enrollment and students are encouraged to videotape the lessons for later study. The courses were being broadcast for twenty-four hours a day and seven days a week via Galaxy III, Transponder 11.

Peter Drucker (1989) also points out that the "age when bigger was better is definitely over. . . . When you look at the global economy, the companies that are doing best are very small specialists." This is true of educational programs as well, and instead of a global university directed by one "hub" administration, what it has and probably will continue to have into the forseeable future is a network of "hubs," some in government, some in business, some in universities. Higher education is already undergoing a transformation as such hubs begin to interconnect electronically. It is not the technology that transforms education; rather, the technology—and perhaps the shock effect of its potential—opens the minds of educators and many students to various new possibilities, ending some of the lethargy and resistance that have preserved so much obsolescence in higher education.

H. G. Wells in his 1938 book, *World Brain*, expressed concern over the enormous waste of human resources that results from outmoded styles of university education. He called for coordinated research and a new kind of less parochial university that could deal more adequately with large-scale global problems. It now appears that what Wells proposed is beginning to happen through electronic interconnections.

A fundamental educational principle is crucial in the global renaissance of higher education predicted by John Sculley (1988): *every person and every culture, as well as every country's educational institutions, have much to teach and much to learn.* All peoples need to share what they have on a two-way basis, as equals—facts, science, knowledge, research methods, wisdom—so that ordinary people as well as scholars and political leaders everywhere can decide for themselves how to develop themselves and their communities for the good of all.

The next chapter reviews efforts to give administrative direction to the emergence of the electronic university and asks how the international electronic university is to be governed. (For case studies on current developments, see Arms 1989, 1990.)

Two

ADMINISTRATIVE STRUCTURE FOR GLOBAL EDUCATION

The force of microelectronics will blow apart all the monopolies,
hierarchies, pyramids and power grids of established . . . society.
George Gilder 1990

The agenda for global higher education begins with questions about
who is to coordinate and regulate electronic courses offered on network
or satellite; who is to set standards, especially when nations and universities disagree; what technology is to be used and how can it be
shared; and who is to arbitrate and decide on such matters as degrees
and exchange of course credits. Also, what kind of administration and
funding can a worldwide electronic university have if it involves many
governments, private colleges, and the teaching programs of business
corporations?

No one yet knows, of course, what the final organizational shape of
global higher education will be and it is premature to recommend administrative models. Ralph Killman (1989), director of the program in
corporate culture at the University of Pittsburgh, says that "the 21st
century will be full of organizational surprises." Much of what he says
about international business is also true of worldwide higher education
and other nonbusiness governance. The traditional forms of organization, such as army or bureaucratic-type hierarchical authority applied to

universities, are no longer working very well. One result is an inability to keep up with changes and a failure "to develop a global perspective."

Around 1980, Killman says, "the world changed . . . as a result of the computer and telecommunication revolutions and the explosion of information." The old style of organizing in divisions, in self-contained departments, and specializations was highly successful at one stage of human development but is no longer functional. Universities now exist in a global context as "the world has become more accessible and change has become more rapid." Educational institutions, as well as business corporations, have reshuffled and improvised. There have been experiments with joint projects and consortia. Similarly, industry has sought to build bridges to research institutions, to government agencies in their own and other countries, and to community groups.

What we see, Killman says, is the emergence of "the network" as the twenty-first century form of institution. No existing university or group of universities and no corporation or government agency is alone likely to dominate and determine the future shape of international electronic education. Its style of organization and governance will develop gradually. Harlan Cleveland (1991), however, argues that an international capacity to act requires "a strong but collective executive", able to perform policy analysis, negotiate consensus on norms and standards, and "blow the whistle when policies aren't carried out."

A variety of governance styles that exist or are proposed are administration by one university that seeks to extend its courses overseas; consortia of universities to exchange courses from country to country; the creation of new international governmental education agencies for distance education; the creation of new organizations—electronic worldwide universities—especially to administer international electronic education; for-profit corporations administering courses in cooperation with educational agencies; and professional organizations themselves offering and administrating electronic courses. (Note the example of medical associations reported by Matheson et al. in Arms 1990.)

As such efforts are examined, it is tempting to conclude that many if not all of these alternatives will remain part of the "kludge" of networks that may govern global electronic education for decades. Unfortunately, governance may be determined by the control of funding rather than on the basis of principle and adequate goals for global higher education.

In addition to university governance structures—administrative hierarchy and faculty senates—a third category of important structures in most universities is the "shadow governments" of the academic disciplines. Electronic overseas education, belonging to extension and continuing education divisions, is not yet a priority for any of the central academic structures in most universities. So its governance may be moving into the hands of forces outside the academic centers of higher education.

In many parts of the world, various associations of universities and agencies are engaged in projects and planning; some of these are the Latin American Network for the Development of Distance Education (REDLAED); the Regional Program on Educational Development (PREDE) of the Organization of American States; the Centro Regional para la Educacion Superior en America Latina el Caribe (CRESALC) of UNESCO; the World Association for the Use of Satellites in Education (WAUSE); the Community of Mediterranean Universities; the Foundation for International TeleEducation (an effort to create a global clearinghouse); the International Federation for Computer-Based Education in Banking; the American Symposium on Research in Distance Education; and the InterAmerican Organization for Higher Education (IOHE) in Canada, involving approximately 325 schools. This list, which could be extended for many pages, suggests the wide variety of types of associations.

Planning groups are asking how the hub/network style may apply to a system for course exchange in which people are electronically connected. At the hub, Killman says, "the traditional division of labor will be replaced by a contemporary division of knowledge organized according to new categories." The hub will be responsible for organizing resources, setting goals, establishing priorities and programs, and keeping the network together.

GOVERNANCE IN THE NTU: ONE MODEL

University consortia came together with business, government, and professional associations to form the National Technological University (NTU). With encouragement of employers, engineering professional groups, and the Department of Defense, several U.S. engineering colleges had started by the mid–1960s (Baldwin 1991) to use instructional TV to offer courses to employees of nearby corporations. These programs were so successful that they set a precedent for "extending high quality advanced-degree education" to students in remote locations. At the same time that space satellites made it possible for TV courses to be offered across North America, there were similar developments in Europe, Australia, China, and elsewhere.

Those programs led in 1984 to the establishment of the NTU, which, by 1991, was a consortium of forty university schools of engineering, with headquarters at Fort Collins, Colorado. By the end of 1990, more than 1,100 distance education students were admitted to graduate degree programs in engineering with the active collaboration of the business corporations that employed them. Most of those receiving Master's degrees from NTU reported that they would not have been able to do so in any other way (Baldwin 1991). As this is written, the NTU has not yet extended its electronic course offerings to other continents, nor has it yet imported courses from Japan, but both possibilities are being examined.

NTU has been widely studied and recommended as a model for administration in global electronic higher education. It is a private, nonprofit corporation, which is governed by a Board of Trustees consisting primarily of industrial executives. In 1991 a headquarters staff of thirty in Fort Collins managed a complex network, both technological and human, that linked forty universities with more than 325 sites where courses were received. Courses were therefore available to sites such as the Argonne National Laboratory, the College Center for Finger Lakes, Kelly Air Force Base, Rochester Community College, Sony Microelectronics Corporation, and AT&T.

Each of those sites "is located at a facility operated by one of 113 sponsoring organizations" and is an example of cooperation among government, university, and business corporations, which suggests to many the pattern that the governance of the emerging international university is going to take (Baldwin 1991).

Credits, Degrees, and Academic Decisions

NTU "is well organized to govern its academic functions, with a graduate faculty of consultants selected from the instructors of each participating institution" (Baldwin 1991). The consultants are organized by subject areas to form Graduate Faculties, "typically with one representative in each discipline from each participating institution." Each faculty has four standing committees: curriculum; admissions, academic standards, and student advising; staffing; and an academic executive committee. A vice president administers all academic functions, with a coordinator in the Fort Collins offices assigned to each graduate faculty.

The curriculum is developed by the faculty representatives in each discipline. The chairperson of the curriculum committee reviews courses that participating universities can make available. Much of the work of faculties and committees is done—and meetings are often held—via computer networking.

Funding

NTU is nearly entirely financed from its students' tuition, which is generally paid by the firms that employ them. This model for funding and offering courses can also work when instruction is offered from one country to another, as illustrated by EuroPace, which serves technical professionals in industry via satellite. When first established, EuroPace was made possible to a large extent by funds from many large corporations. They did not so much make grants as pledge large sums to be paid as tuition for students who were employees of those corporations. EuroPace, however, in contrast to NTU, offers only noncredit instruction.

NTU would prefer to have its success judged by "the magnitude of its credit services to students" (Baldwin 1991b). As a model for governance and funding however, NTU attracts attention because of the fact that after six years of operation it was expecting total revenues of $13.5 million for the 1990–91 school year, an increase of more than two million over the previous year (Heller 1991). And if present trends continue, by 1994–95, NTU will offer more Master's degrees in engineering than any other institution in the United States. NTU also had some 65,000 non-credit enrollments during the 1989–90 school year.

COMMONWEALTH OF LEARNING

Distance education existing outside North America is largely now conducted by government-funded "open universities," which may offer courses via radio or TV or increasingly in combination with computer and other technologies (Lundin 1988). Electronic higher education programs have been developed in thirty countries including many in the Third World. For example, over 250,000 such students were reported in Thailand (Shane 1989).

Therefore, a major alternative to the NTU approach to funding and governance would logically be a cooperative arrangement between— and sharing of courses among—such distance education programs. This idea is now a possibility through the Commonwealth of Learning (COL), created by the heads of the fifty governments (of what was once known as the British Commonwealth) to expand opportunities for students in those countries through distance education. The Commonwealth heads of government, who met in Vancouver, Canada, in 1987, decided to establish a facility, using distance education techniques, through which colleges, universities, and other institutions in Commonwealth countries could work cooperatively. The goal was to "foster a network—not an institution—to share expertise" (Lundin 1988).

The COL's long-term aim is to make it possible for "any learner, anywhere in the Commonwealth [to take] any distance teaching programme from any bona fide college or university in the Commonwealth." This implies going "beyond the narrow concept of physical movement of students from one country to another into a much wider concept of the mobility of ideas, knowledge, and learning . . . to free knowledge from national boundaries and ideological confines and to share it through an ambitious exchange of educational resources" (Lundin 1988). The global expansion of communication channels can make this possible; therefore the COL affirms commitments to expand the opportunity for personal choices to the student, to exchange experience and expertise (including technology) among colleges and educational institutions, and to make more quality education available.

To achieve these goals, the COL set up an impressive international board, headed in 1991 by Lord Briggs, chancellor of the British Open University. The founding president was Professor James Maraj, formerly vice-chancellor of the University of the South Pacific and Commonwealth assistant general secretary, now head of education grants in India. Canada and the province of British Columbia gave twelve million dollars to establish a coordinating headquarters in Vancouver, the Commonwealth Center for Distance Education. Other countries in the Commonwealth also contributed, including developing countries such as Brunei, India, and Nigeria. The COL has therefore been well funded in its exploratory and organizational phase and it has before it the prospect of enlarged funding from Commonwealth countries.

Together these countries are creating what begins to look like a "consumer cooperative" to coordinate existing "distance learning programs," to strengthen them, and to expand international electronic education through COL auspices. While the COL does not limit its programs to higher education only, it draws on the resources and experience of the "open universities" and open learning institutions such as the Open Polytechnic (New Zealand) and the Open Learning Agency (Canada). Focusing as it does on human resource development, especially for Third World nations, the COL provides not just a second chance but perhaps the only chance for many students to obtain high-quality education and training (Steward 1991).

The COL is particularly challenging to those seeking to fund other alternatives. The COL's fifty or so member countries represent a wide spectrum of cultures, available resources, and infrastructures. It seeks to provide information to all Commonwealth countries through the most effective means available. This necessitates a proactive policy, seeking out the needs of individual countries as well as responding to incoming requests. It builds upon extensive experience, such as that of the British Open University, which is open to all students, regardless of academic qualification, is open to new teaching methodologies, is open to students at home, wherever they may be, and is available at any time of life or of the year (Pelton 1990); and that of the universities in the South Pacific and West Indies, "which employ satellite-derived telecommunication systems as a fundamental part of their programmes across . . . oceans"

(Commonwealth of Learning 1990). For example, the University of the South Pacific has provided, via satellite, distance students with quality courses at a third or less of the cost to on-campus students and the success rate is high.

UNIVERSITY OF THE WORLD

A major effort to bring some organization and direction into emerging worldwide higher education is the University of the World (UW) project. It was created and incorporated in California in 1983 by some of the officials who earlier were instrumental in creating EDUCOM, a nonprofit computing projects consortium of six hundred or so universities, first in North America but now in many countries; and in establishing its computer network (BITCOM), a major component of the networking that is moving to interconnect all the world's universities.

The UW began with a communication endorsed by the U.S. Department of State to most of the major countries of the world, inviting all governments to affiliate. Each nation was requested to establish a national council of the UW that would bring together and give representation to all of the governmental and private agencies in that nation that are or should be involved in an international electronic exchange of educational resources.

The UW now exists with an international board of distinguished directors, has units or councils developing in many countries, and is financially supported by an increasing number of governments. In a sense it follows a top-down approach, beginning with governments and official educational agencies of the participating nations, in contrast to some other organizations that seek to promote the international electronic university idea by beginning from the bottom up, by experimenting with courses offered from a university in one country to a student or school in another.

UW materials describe it as a "global umbrella," covering the academic activities of the nations, a unique international coalition of scholars and students, and nongovernmental, nonpolitical, nonprofit. "It is designed to employ a total systems approach to facilitate, integrate, and implement a range of educational and research activities using electronic media in various countries" (UW 1991).

The UW proposes an electronic style of administration: "Multiway electronic network connections link University of the World offices in each country with every other national office and the Central Office." It is hoped that this network will function like a central nervous system to unite and integrate all the components of the UW globally. "It will involve various media including telephone, fax, telex, cable, compact disk, videodisc, satellite, computer network, radio, packet radio, video and ultimately two-way interactive video."

THE GLOSAS/GU PROJECT

Where the UW began by soliciting funds and support from governments, and the NTU began with support from U.S. government agencies and business corporations, the Global University (GU) project of the Systems Analysis and Simulation (GLOSAS) organization headed by Takeshi Utsumi has sought to stimulate international electronic university development by beginning first with demonstrations to show what is possible. As educators on five continents have become involved in these demonstrations of electronic exchange from continent to continent, they see what can happen and become persuaded to cooperate and participate (Utsumi 1989).

As this is written in 1991, neither the UW or GLOSAS/GU has as yet actually offered a course from one continent to another, but GLOSAS is extensively involved in facilitating the efforts of universities that wish to do so. GLOSAS has helped with the negotiations and demonstrations necessary to establish "sister university" relationships with schools in other countries. GLOSAS "global classroom" demonstrations (see chapter 9), such as the one at the Fifteenth World Conference of the International Council for Distance Education, in Venezuela, November 1990, have helped GLOSAS discover technological, regulatory, economic, and marketing impediments that need to be removed to enable the emergence of a worldwide electronic university system. GLOSAS has also devoted major research efforts to finding ways to cut costs so that electronic course exchange can be possible for countries with limited financial resources.

In the 1970s GLOSAS began the political work, which it still continues, of getting government regulations changed and legal barriers removed. This made it possible for U.S. data communication networks to be extended overseas, first to Japan. This step was essential to make possible course exchange and free electronic access—through computer conferencing, television, and so forth—from one country to another for educational purposes. The work of GLOSAS therefore rests on a solid foundation of appreciation for this accomplishment. The easing of restrictions, as the European Community followed suit, has made possible a wide variety of electronic educational experiments and programs (Utsumi, Rossman, and Rosen 1989.)

GLOSAS and its GU project planners act as if—for the present at least—governance and organizational plans should be kept open and fluid so that all kinds of networking can continue, perhaps for a long time, until an authentic style of networking for global university governance can emerge.

ALTERNATIVE ADMINISTRATION

The term "alternative technology" is frequently used for simple, low-cost projects that are affordable to the Third World. Can these similarly be "low-cost alternative administration" in a global networking system? There has not been adequate Third World representation at organizational meetings of the University of the World or the GLOSAS Global University project because travel from continent to continent is so expensive.

One of the technicians at a UW annual meeting where delegates from China, Russia, and many Third World areas were represented, asked: "If we can exchange significant courses online, through computer and television conferencing, why can't all the meetings and administrative work be done that way also? How long must we wait before university people, at least all those who have access to a node connecting to a computer network, are invited to attend these meetings online?" The UW has announced that, in principle, that organization does intend to have as many of its meetings as possible on computer networks. The October 1991 UW Annual Meeting at EDUCOM in San Diego had a session that university people in Latin America could attend via teleconference.

Thus large numbers of people, in universities in many countries, could participate in committee planning and coordination and in global business and administrative meetings at affordable costs. Then perhaps projects and responsibilities can be divided among many universities and agencies. At a meeting of the Foundation for Instructional Tele-Education, for example, it was suggested that perhaps the staff of the Commonwealth of Learning might serve as a provisional secretariat, and that other international agencies would each assume one area of work, much as each participating university in every country might provide a course or two.

ADMINISTRATIVE IDEAS FROM CORPORATIONS

The experience of multinational corporations may also strongly influence how administrative issues will be solved, since electronic higher education involves universities in a system of world trade. International corporations must function in the midst of the same complexities that face the worldwide university such as

- time differences over large geographic areas;

- the problem of language, soon perhaps being solved by computer translation systems;
- setting priorities in a situation in which cultures and national interests and needs greatly vary;
- the problem of strategic planning, as, for example, in deciding what courses to make available, when, where, and to whom;
- the problem of degree credit, course development, and other arrangements with cooperating (and noncooperating) universities;
- the problems of technology and telecommunication standards and regulations; and
- questions of quality of courses and software, educational standards, diploma mills, policies.

We have already noted that business corporations are a major component of the emerging worldwide electronic university. Electronic training programs for employees such as IBM's in-company satellite education system constitute one of the largest segments of higher education today, not counting the corporation purchase of instruction from NTU or EuroPace. Private corporation education networks are operated by such companies as General Motors, J. C. Penney, Ford, Walmart, and Federal Express (see Pelton 1900). Many of these corporate systems are far ahead of higher education institutions in technological sophistication of the instruction and in its quantity (Brock 1990).

FUNDING FOR GLOBAL ELECTRONIC EDUCATION

Organizationally, the UW began on a sound foundation with the endorsement and support of major governments and of many major international agencies in education. Yet although it has raised funds from foundations, corporations, memberships, and government grants, it had by 1991 not yet succeeded in underwriting a budget adequate for the accomplishment of its task. No matter how sound in theory and approach, the UW and GU are in competition with all universities that have budgets to raise, and with all of the other varied kinds of educational organizations doing electronic education. Since nearly everything is dependent on money, the first and most urgent question is how to secure long-term sustained funding, not so much for the exchange of lectures and courses as for administration, experimentation, and development.

A Global Endowment?

Some propose a major endowment effort, an international campaign to raise several hundred million dollars from corporations, government agencies, wills, private gifts, and foundations. The emerging electronic university has no wealthy alumni, yet donors often endow schools they did not attend and some wealthy donors might be intrigued by the idea of an endowment to aid the undeveloped nations.

A UN Agency?

Some hope that the governments of the world will set up the administrative structures for global electronic higher education as a major UN agency, perhaps like UNESCO, with a budget from all nations that is at least adequate for a coordinating umbrella, providing for essential meetings and publications, especially catalogs and directories. The Commonwealth of Learning, officially involving many governments, may be a step in that direction.

A Cooperative Agency?

Something like a "Global Community Chest" might seek to coordinate fund-raising by developing a plan to share jointly raised funds on an agreed percentage basis. Fund-raising might be strengthened by an international telethon that would seek to interconnect as many of the world's higher education institutions as possible. TV that inspires millions to contribute for hungry children might also inspire millions to contribute funds to aid educationally underprivileged people.

Tuition Sharing?

When students are able to pay tuition for their on-line courses a percentage can go to the worldwide system. Elliot Washor and Deborah Couture tell of a distance learning system which is "revenue-generating and self-sustaining." A formula, as in Thailand, has been devised for tuition fees from students to "ensure that the program will pay for itself" and not be dependent on government funding.

Funds from Cooperating Universities:

Most universities, even the most well endowed, do not have large amounts of money that can be contributed to international budgets. Indeed, as this is written, many American universities have had to cut their information services budgets by more than 30 percent. However, once overhead or "umbrella" administrative structures exist and are funded, many universities and students can pay for lectures and courses they need. Many colleges can share fees for on-line courses that students are willing to pay for. Despite their limited budgets, universities can contribute lectures, courses, publicity, and some administrative and technological services. Many institutions could each assume a small share of a global program, as they do in NTU. Many electronic education projects can be carried out with contributed services.

Furthermore, Edward Yarrish (1991) points out that the electronic university can bring significant economies and growth to universities. Compared to on-campus buildings that are expensive to build and maintain, the "electronic classroom via modem ... can be used 24 hours a day, 7 days a week, 365 days a year. Setting up a new electronic classroom can be done in a few minutes with software commands." He points out further that computers and electronics are an area of world economy where productivity significantly increases, in contrast to other higher education, which continues to increase in cost each year "with little change in the product." Joseph Pelton (1990) points out that in the United States public school electronic-based tele-education is already "a multi-billion dollar enterprise."

Corporations, when partners in global education, can also contribute staff services, the use of technological infrastructure and programs as well as funds. Perhaps many of them would, with a proper plan and negotiations, continue to contribute free satellite and communications time, especially during hours of the day and week when their facilities are underused.

Consortia of schools can better negotiate for special rates from common carriers. Hardware and software equipment could be obtained at much better prices if jointly purchased for many Third World institutions by a cooperative agency such as the UW or the World Association for the Use of Satellites in Education (WAUSE). Established at a conference in Italy in June 1991, WAUSE is a project of the Community of 128 Mediterranean Universities, although its founding members also include the NTU in the United States, the International Association for Continuing Engineering Education (IACEE), and many others than extend far beyond the Mediterranean.

Whoever administers international education budgets with tight fiscal restraints will find it hard to set priorities. Should funds first of all go to the Third World? What share of budget should be allocated to students and faculty themselves to spend on "appropriate technology" such as fax machines and computers? Should such a consortium spend large sums putting its own satellite into orbit and developing an infrastructure system or should it rent (and in the Third World, borrow) infrastructure developed by business and for other purposes?

Money is wasted if there is no agreement on the content of courses. Education money is mismanaged and not well used when there are "no clearly stated objectives, no philosophy for managing a multi-billion dollar business . . . no accountability for academic achievement; . . . no standard cost-accounting system" (Perot 1989).

There are many other programs and organizations that offer courses to another country, or that plan to do so soon, that would be described here but for space limitations; for example, the Electronic University Network, the International Space University, the International School of Information Management, and individual universities and consortia of schools. The next chapter discusses the possibilities of Third World participation in the emerging electronic university in spite of financial and other limitations.

Three

EDUCATION FOR ALL THE WORLD

> Zaghloul Morsy, editor of the UNESCO journal, refers to distance
> education as a quiet revolution... it can provide education at con-
> siderably lower cost, and it makes access to educational opportunities
> possible for many people.
>
> Armando Villarroel, former vice-rector
> of Venezuela's open university, in Clark 1989

Neither the entire world nor any one nation can be healthy and thrive
while large percentages of people lack adequate education for health
care, jobs, and survival (see Tessler 1991). What is not yet clear, however,
is the extent to which programs of electronic higher education can help
bring the necessary opportunities and quality into every community,
school, college, university, and research program in the world.

Shortages of education, like shortages of food, are often a matter of
politics (Sharma 1986), but there is also the crucial question of what can
be afforded. The quality of higher education in Brazil, for example, is
reported to have declined with the deterioration of the economy and
the presence of huge foreign debt. Brazilians asked how they could
reverse the trend without significant outside educational help (Hart
1988).

We must not expect too much from technology, which often creates
as many new problems as solutions, yet radio and television have been

effectively used in many parts of the world to bring education to places where it was lacking (see Moore and Clark 1989a). In fact, such technologies may be the best and most affordable way to bring higher quality education to many of the world's deprived areas. To improve the quality of existing schools, education via TV and computer networking is not used to replace local teachers but to help them do a better job by enlarging the resources available to them and by training them to use such resources.

Many of the educational packages now available for broadcast in Europe and North America would not be acceptable to other cultures or adequate to meet the needs of many other countries. Officials of the British Open University, however, have pointed to a "vast store of educational programming" that educators in other countries could adapt for use. The quality and adaptability of such materials are greatly enhanced by computer technology that makes possible interactive two-way participation, where TV and radio have largely been one-way communication. New tools also make it possible to aid educators in each country and culture in creating and adapting the types of educational programs that are most needed and that could be most effective there.

Many people, however, especially in developing countries, worry that the best intentioned international electronic education, much like entertainment television and commercial films, may become a new form of cultural and economic colonialism, especially if rich industrialized countries dominate the emerging worldwide electronic university.

Paul Lauby, for Global Educational Associates (1987), points out that the Asian university itself is largely a Western import, founded by people with Western values, world views, and the concerns of Western civilization. Often, instead of educating people to meet the real needs of their countries, these "exported" universities turn out Western-style lawyers and bureaucrats in a much greater supply than is required. So there is an urgent need in the emerging electronic university to recover indigenous history, value systems, religious insights, art, music, and literature as the foundation for higher education in each culture. For example, Lauby asks, what would Indian higher education be like if it issued from the mainsprings of Indian thought and cultural traditions, and if it were solidly rooted in the soul of India?

This is not, however, an either/or situation. In Asia and elsewhere, higher education must also be oriented to international problems and to the emerging global society to prepare a new generation for worldwide citizenship. This will require a "partnership style of education" among the nations.

TWO-WAY EXCHANGE OF EDUCATION

Where one-way radio, films, television, and videotape have been largely dominated by Europe, North America, and more recently Japan, the new computer-managed interactive and two-way communication technologies can be an antidote to colonialism and authoritarianism everywhere. These two-way communication technologies make possible more of a partnership in which economically underdeveloped countries can trade lectures, courses, and data bases on their history and culture for the latest scientific lectures from other countries.

When we ask how poorer nations are to pay for their share of a worldwide electronic education system, the following must be held in mind: "Developing countries possess extensive . . . information sources which can be translated into tangible benefits to developed countries" (Vagianos 1988). The data they have can be traded for needed courses and information, and developed nations can thus benefit from "new sources of political and economic information" and from insights from other cultures.

The electronic university need not ask a student in Indonesia or France to choose between a traditional course on campus or an electronic course from overseas. The traditional course, with lectures and discussion on campus, can be supplemented and enriched by some videotape lectures by a distant specialist, and "electronic classroom discussion" between students in France and a specialist lecturer in Indonesia or vice versa. A videotaped lecture may come by mail or can be downloaded from a satellite if it is important to have the most up-to-date information immediately. The class can view the videotape and discuss it, and each individual student can review it, over and over if necessary, to cope with linguistic limitations and formulate questions before the class meets electronically with the expert in another country for questions and discussion. The local instructor can counsel and guide members of a class to profit from such electronically provided resources.

EDUCATION FOR ALL AGES AND NEEDS

Many open university courses use radio and TV to extend education and bring better quality into primary and secondary schools as well as colleges. UN consultant Rashmi Mayur of India insists that electronic opportunities must be provided for "everyone, wherever that person may be." For him the goal of the emerging worldwide electronic university must be to extend all significant kinds of literacy (cultural, technical, mathematical, scientific) to every human being in the world, never for a moment neglecting the illiterate villagers of Asia or Africa.

At first it would seem that primary and secondary education would only be provided within the boundaries of a country, and not by "electronic providers" from outside. The goal of heightened quality, however, involves an internationalization of educational resources, especially in science and foreign language. John Southworth at the the University of Hawaii, for example, has conducted a decade of imaginative experiments and demonstrations, via a computer network, to connect primary and secondary school pupils with similar age group classrooms in other countries. Research and experience show that high quality education can be provided via new technologies where it cannot otherwise be affordable or available (see Moore and Clark 1989a and 1989b).

AVOID A NEW COLONIALISM?

In principle, the leaders of the emerging electronic higher education consortia are planning for boards of directors that are broadly representative of developing countries; that will therefore be committed to quality education for the Third World as well as for all others; that will make it possible for educators and students to define their own needs and interests; and that will give priority to promoting kinds of education that people in each country want and prefer.

Protection against colonialism is stressed in the statements of purpose and philosophy of Global Education Associates (GEA), which operates in seventy-eight countries, as well as in the purpose statements of the UW and GLOSAS/GU project and other programs and groups seeking to give some leadership to the emerging electronic university. GEA, for example, has sought to define the cultural context for global education, taking account of such factors as regional history giving way to an era of global history; the emergence of an interrelated multifaceted global economy; the coming into existence of a worldwide interstate system that is eroding traditional boundaries between domestic and international politics; a world culture emerging on top of traditional local and regional cultures; human beings everywhere taking new account of the ecological unity of the planet; and international networking in industry, politics, and education and expanding international institutions.

With these factors in mind, GEA thus proposes that the foundation for global education rests on new common understandings, such as the realization that respecting others who are different enriches rather than diminishes each of us; that common human needs and dreams underlie cultural differences; and that the globally educated person will be one who acts *intelligently* to promote a more humane domestic and foreign policy; *compassionately* to contribute to the solution of humanity's common problems; *realistically* to seek to eradicate hunger and improve the quality of life for all; *vigorously* to try to promote justice; *conscientiously* to aim to become involved in the peaceful resolution of conflict with the goal of outlawing war; and *responsibly* to curb wasteful consumption of the world's resources.

SOME PROPOSED PRINCIPLES

Those planning the GLOSAS/Global University project, in part building upon these GEA values and principles, have published a booklet in Italy (see DeMaio and Utsumi 1991) that proposes guidelines for the emerging electronic university. That draft statement on educational principles was prepared by a committee chaired by Professor Stephen Rosen of the College of Staten Island for a consultation in April 1988 at the headquarters of Global Education Associates. The proposals, summarized below, suggest a philosophy of worldwide electronic higher education that gives priority to the needs and concerns of developing countries.

Focus on the needs of all. The primary goal of the emerging electronic university must be a cross-cultural and global initiative to promote the sort of global higher education that will advance peace and international understanding as "absolutely essential to the survival of humanity on our planet." A much higher percentage of the world's people must be provided with education—including skills to earn a decent living—that is adequate to make possible long-term prosperity, world friendship, peace, and participation in democratic global governance.

A partnership. The initiative in the electronic university should be in the hands of the individual student, with a partnership of educational institutions, government agencies, and industry finding and providing resources to make it possible for all people in the world to obtain whatever education they need. When striving for universal literacy and seeking to make available the very best educational resources to all, priority should be given to the goal of serving especially those who cannot otherwise adequately participate in the emerging global economy and information age.

Freedom for education. Global higher education, especially through electronic connections, must in all societies promote freedom of speech and freedom of thought. In a world of parochial and competing universities that are often controlled by the priorities of governments, industry, and the military, those who finance educational programs must understand that "control does not follow financing and must affirm the freedom of the university in teaching and research."

Priority to moral principles. A partnership of many kinds of institutions and individuals "must seek to challenge and question the goals and purposes of those who provide services and of those who use them." For example, the emerging electronic university would reject partnership with a government that wants to use it to get access to technology for war and oppression of its own citizens or those of other countries. Even if the aim appears idealistic, electronic higher education can follow the

United Nations, for example, in asking all participants to affirm and support internationally agreed-upon aims, purposes, and long-range goals. From its beginning, the electronic university should affirm its intention to support curriculum and activities that can promote world harmony and human needs, rejecting any courses or programs likely to be used for the purposes of exploitation, aggression, or evil, destructive ends.

Help humanity meet critical challenges. The electronic university should make every effort to help humanity avert widespread calamity, undertaking research to help solve problems such as the homelessness, hunger, disease, and pollution that now face many if not all countries. Affirming that academic freedom should be for research as well as for teaching, those taking initiative in global higher education should work diligently to help make it possible for researchers in important fields of knowledge to collaborate across international boundaries, for example, using computer networking and computer bulletin boards to coordinate their efforts. Bringing many minds together to explore new alternatives for solving global problems and for the management of complexity can bring enlarged collective intelligence to bear upon all major global issues.

Free global access to information. All officials, faculty, and students related to the worldwide electronic university should affirm "the principle of free global access and exchange of information and educational resources" and the goal of an on-line and, in time, an open CD-ROM-type satellite library, available to any school, educational institution, or individual anywhere in the world.

A rich interplay of disciplines, cultures, and schools of thought. Courses and lectures that are exchanged should come from centers of excellence recognized for high quality, should seek to be based on the most up-to-date research and methods, should have a clear relevance to the needs of the student and his or her culture, should respond as rapidly as possible to newly emerging and changing knowledge, and should represent types and contents of training not widely and/or easily available through other means and nearby institutions. In other words, the international electronic university, whatever its manifestations, rather than being competitive, should seek to improve and complement existing higher education institutions, providing outlets and resources on a global scale. A highly significant cultural interchange can be possible through kinds of electronic cooperation that can enable a dynamic synthesis of oneness and diversity. In contrast to the fear of depersonalization caused by technology, a process of sharing and dialog should emphasize neither cultural uniformity nor cultural difference, but should favor "a dynamic synthesis of oneness and diversity, a trans-cultural unity-in-difference."

More than intellect. Enlarging the goal of improving the quality of excellence of education everywhere "should involve the heart as well as the mind." The emerging electronic university should become "not merely personal but trans-personal" so as to address humankind's present need for a sharing of minds and hearts across personal and cultural barriers. To meet the needs of all the world's children for health care, education, food, and clean air and water, feelings must be shared as well as ideas.

CAN ALL NATIONS AFFORD TO PARTICIPATE?

The question of how individual students can afford a fair share in the emerging worldwide electronic university is given one answer in Latin America. Some educators there point out that hundreds of their students can participate in electronically offered courses with the money it would cost to send one student to Europe or North America. Also, there are ways to make the electronic exchange of education affordable through reducing communication costs. Where communication infrastructure is often lacking, as in parts of Africa, packet radio may be especially useful (Quarterman 1990). It has already been used there by the U. S. Peace Corps, Volunteers in Technical Assistance (VITA), and the Canadian University Service Overseas. A usable system, described by John Quarterman, can be put together for less than five hundred dollars. Such packet-satellite methods, developed at the University of North Texas, using NASA's Applied Technology Satellite, have already used radio to connect personal computers in Texas with Samoa, Hawaii, and Tonga for education purposes (Utsumi, Rossman and Rosen 1989). In 1991 there are official requests for permission to launch a constellation of low-earth satellites so that small, modestly priced, hand-held and battery-powered portable telephones could be used anywhere in the world for inexpensive links to computer networks (Cowlan 1991).

As an extensive international technological communications infrastructure is developed for other purposes, such as for use by medicine and industry, education can piggyback upon it, often using borrowed facilities. For example, there were negotiations for a Central American network to piggyback on the global IBM network, but the effort was not successful (Quarterman 1990). The next chapter tells about computer networks that are increasingly interconnecting all the world's universities. It was reported at the second annual UW board meeting that these connections have penetrated the developing countries much more than realized—even if some of the connections have been like the householder who taps into cable TV without permission. A former president of Costa Rica reported at the UW meeting that all Central American universities, and one in the Caribbean, were now electronically interconnected, and that plans were underway to connect also with South America. They were pushing ahead, he said, to exchange courses and other programs with the realization that together they could accomplish a quality of education that none of them could afford alone.

David Hughes (1991) describes how at the time of the Tiananmen Square events a laptop Toshiba computer and a modem with two alligator clips attached to an ancient Chinese rotary phone were used to connect students at a remote university in China with the outside world. Hughes finds that new high-speed modems can overcome the limitations of old poor-quality telephone lines that have up to this point often limited on-line education in some countries (see Applegate 1991, Omnet 1988 on how to outwit even the most antiquated phone system).

Lewis M. Branscomb (1989) reminds us that as in "research telecollaboration, distance learning leverages economies of scale through the sharing of a valuable resource, increases productivity [by reducing both travel time and costs] and compensates for isolation." Harlan Cleveland (1991) points out that the poverty of many underdeveloped countries does not result from a lack of resources but from a lack of learning, the ability to use resources.

Despite forthcoming successful ways to reduce drastically the costs of exchanging courses and lectures, some countries still cannot afford even the initial demonstrations and experimentation, and all in the Third World must wonder what a worldwide electronic university can provide that is worth the cost.

WORTHWHILE EXPENDITURES

What courses or offerings are worth pursuing? It was reported at a conference in Asia (Sharma 1986) that 10 percent of World Bank projects have involved distance education for four purposes:

1. to enrich face-to-face teaching;
2. to upgrade the qualifications and skills of teachers;
3. to provide instruction where not enough teachers were available locally;
4. and to provide instruction where teachers or the needed education could not otherwise be provided.

There is still a bit of colonialism in that statement, even when the distance education is only internal as when a nation connects to deprived rural areas for its own citizens. Existing universities are rarely equal partnerships between those who give and those who receive, or partnerships between various disciplines to serve the poor and illiterate. So even as new and more idealistic long-range goals are provided for the worldwide university, the present limited systems will continue to expand and develop, at least until major governments begin to provide large sums for a truly global system of higher education.

Some of the electronic university's most important early Third World developments may well be the exchange of courses among Spanish-speaking countries; and some countries in Africa and Asia that use English may first exchange lectures and courses among themselves with some extensions from England, Australasia, and North America.

ELECTRONICALLY OFFER WHAT KINDS OF COURSES?

We can get a picture of the first kinds of course offerings by looking at a copy of *Satellite Learning*, a sort of TV guide to courses now electronically available in North America to public schools, high schools and universities, as well as to individuals at home. The first significant electronic higher education course offerings in North America are in medicine, engineering, and computer science. The first significant exchange of courses for advanced degrees between North America and Asia are likely to be in engineering, the NTU already having demonstrated how to do it and how it can be funded by corporations.

So also, the best courses offered globally may first be in areas where business corporations want to upgrade the education of their employees. Researchers at AT&T's National Teletraining Center (Chute, Balthazar, and Poston 1989) examined the effectiveness of such education using a "combination of information technology and communications services." They found it to be a cost-effective method of providing quality training for AT&T employees. They reported that almost no American universities were actually offering the skills courses that many corporations need or at the desired time and place (see Kearsley 1985 on methods). The International School of Information Management, offering only graduate degrees, has been established to serve learners worldwide "through the technology it trains them to manage: computers and computer networks" (Brock 1990). However it is done, it is increasingly clear that business corporations are going to be major partners in the emerging electronics university.

Greg Kearsley (1985) uses the term "distributed education," learning essentially independent of time and space, for the new style of education effectively used by corporations. "The design and administration of distributed learning is very different from traditional educational approaches," he says. Other higher education programs can profit from this extensive and successful experience. Joseph Pelton (1990), however, warns that corporate training programs put the needs of the corporation ahead of what the learner may most need and want to know. Nevertheless the international networks set up by corporations for the continuing and continuous education of their employees are likely to be models of how a worldwide electronic university can function.

The course offerings listed in *Satellite Learning* magazine show what people—business, government and educators—now want badly enough to pay for

- computer and electronic networking courses (it is perhaps only natural that students of computer science would be the first to get access to on-line courses and would first use them for information they need and want for their own study);
- engineering courses and some advanced science;
- medical education, including community health;
- some teacher training, especially on how to use the new technologies;
- business training (for corporations, but also for college schools of business entrepreneurship); and
- agriculture, the teaching and research necessary to feed the people of the world.

When I have asked university and government officials in Asia and Latin America what they might like to receive from an electronic university, these same six areas are the course areas and library resources mentioned. Their faculty and their graduate students would like access to the latest technical and scientific data in areas most crucial to their personal careers and to meet basic needs in their countries.

When one looks at what courses individual overseas students tend to take via computer conferencing, a similar pattern emerges. An examination of present trends suggests to me that there will be a gradual increase in the number of adventurous individuals in many countries who experiment with taking a course from a distant university via computer conference. This adventuring may make significant contributions to the long-range goal of making it possible for any student in the world to take any needed course electronically if it is not available otherwise.

It can be a great mistake, however, to see the emerging worldwide university only as extending electronically to other countries courses that are now being offered domestically. The enlargement of course offerings from one country to another may in the next few years consist of teleconferencing to university classes or to clusters of students who come together at a remote site. Such groups of individuals, meeting at a nearby primary school to receive a course electronically, can share costs that, even if subsidized by a government, would be difficult or impossible for any one student to afford alone.

The next chapter introduces the enabling technology for those who are not already familiar with it.

Four

THE CHALLENGE OF TECHNOLOGY

> The existing web of computer, telephone, broadcast, and other kinds
> of networks does not (yet) constitute the ... powerful infrastruc-
> ture—no more than the thousands of U.S. dirt roads in the early
> 1900s made a national highway system.
>
> Michael Dertouzos 1991

To help those who know little about the technologies used for electronic
exchange of education, this chapter summarizes some proposals—using
Latin America as an example—for what may be most useful and appropriate for both advanced and developing nations. Technologies are
changing so rapidly, however, that what is written in 1991 will soon be
out of date.

Those who have not had time to keep up with technology are nevertheless increasingly affected and challenged by the electronic/digital developments that appear to be transforming education. Perhaps the most
important aspect of the technology for a global higher education network
is not any one component, such as increasingly versatile and powerful
computers, but rather the interconnection of technologies on a global
scale. Combinations into more comprehensive tools can make possible
some kinds of research, instruction, and educational experimentation
on a scale never before possible.

Some large and very powerful (and often costly) technologies are involved in the reshaping of higher education, for example, artificial intelligence/expert system software, and simulations like the FUGI representation of the world's economies at Soka University in Japan. Many of these, however, are too expensive to be used by poorer countries in the near future. Combinations of much simpler technologies are what is creating an educational revolution for them.

International course sharing initially involves such technologies as video- and audiotapes, computer networks, TV, and packet radio and telephones (see Gilder 1990). Many of these are currently used in conventional on-campus courses as well. Greg Kearsley (1985), for example, reminds us that continuing education for engineers, cosponsored by engineering societies, often involves many kinds of courses on videotape. Such videotapes now become one effective component in a larger mix, empowered by interactive two-way participation and can be used for the benefit of a class or of an individual, self-directed learner. In any case, worldwide electronic education begins with the telephone, television, and computer communications systems, increasingly accessible to all via satellite.

SATELLITES

The global communications system has been transformed by satellites that "provide medical service" and "educate millions of students in remote villages" so that "half the world's population can be linked together live via satellite at any time of day or night" (Pelton and Howkins 1987). That percentage will escalate.

The International Telecommunications Satellite Organization (INTELSAT) operates a global satellite system for public use. It is "structured as a global collective" (Pelton and Howkins 1987). Its operations began in 1971 and by 1987 its fifteen satellites were used by 170 countries. It has commercial and other competitors, and also faces competition from fiberglass cables, which are beginning to interconnect the world.

As a kind of public service utility, INTELSAT has been required to serve the world at reasonable prices. Its Project SHARE has provided some free satellite time for education and health services, making it possible by 1987 for seventy countries to use this service, including China, which has provided electronic education to a million students. INTELSAT's Business Service (IBS), providing digital services to low-cost terminals, is also being explored for international education.

Television became an important component of distance education in part because of INTELSAT's demonstration of reliability. An effective two-way satellite system for exchanging educational resources integrates a satellite and an earth (receiving/sending) station. Although most people think of the earth station as a dish-type antenna now so often seen in the yards or on the roofs of schools, an earth station can be in a mobile van or even in a portable pack as small as a suitcase (see description by Nosaka in Pelton and Howkins 1987).

It is expensive to wire the earth with the optical fiber cables able to carry the volume of sophisticated material required for global-scale research. The companies that operate cables must "charge by the mile" to recover costs. High frequency radio, though much cheaper, is often unreliable. Satellites can therefore have a great advantage in reduced cost. A flexible pricing policy could be adjusted to serve more effectively the educational institutions of the underdeveloped world (Hudson and Jussawalla 1987).

Indonesia was the first developing country to own its own satellite system. It has been used to link eleven university campuses on different islands for distance education and teacher training "to improve educational quality" (Hudson and Jussawalla 1987). The University of the South Pacific and the University of the West Indies have similarly served education needs in several widely scattered island countries. India early used "NASA's ATS 6 satellite to deliver educational programming to more than 2,500 villages."

Affordable options with a mix of technologies can be provided to developing countries. Universities using satellites can, for example, use full-motion television for video conferencing; audio and computer conferencing; computer conferencing through a digital network; or audiographics (combinations of technology such as slow-scan TV, facsimile, and electronic blackboards or text on computer screens). Satellites are expected to develop in remarkable and probably unexpected ways in the next decades. In addition to sending many more courses at a time, they may then provide three-dimensional, two-way television and broadband services that can greatly empower international education "as phased array antennas . . . create very high-powered beams with low sidelobes." It is therefore unlikely that optical fiber cables will replace satellites since "air and vacuum are cheaper." Satellite technology breakthroughs should soon bring the price down to "less than ten percent of current levels" (Pelton and Howkins 1987).

A very expensive type of educational exchange, which has been demonstrated between the United States and the Soviet Union, uses regular commercial-type television. The Japanese government in January 1989, announced a plan to put into orbit a geo-synchronous telecommunications satellite, sometime between 1992 and 1994, to be used only for "non-profit purposes of international education, exchange of academic researches, information transfer to medicine, etc." (*Nihon Keisai Shim-*

bun, Jan. 12, 1989). While commercial-type TV technology is helpful from time to time so that members of a class in different locations can get acquainted with each other, it is unnecessary for good education.

Less expensive is slow-scan television (SSTV), which sends the signal via the ordinary telephone system to be viewed one frame at a time. New York University, for example, has used SSTV to instruct graduate students in Puerto Rico. Where full motion video (commercial TV) via satellite from continent to continent costs several thousand dollars per hour, SSTV goes at regular long-distance telephone rates. Many educators do not realize the excellent quality of graphics that can now be sent via ordinary telephone connections, even with only one line. When video images, which can include print and graphic information, are exchanged during a class, SSTV delivers precision visual images over narrowband telephone-type communications channels without the installation of special circuits. There have already been many demonstrations of the practicality and usefulness of SSTV in distance education, and there is every likelihood that its quality and sophistication will increase.

BLANKING INTERVAL

Now that regular broadcast TV exists nearly everywhere in the world, an alternative method for using TV stations for education has been demonstrated by the Public Broadcasting Service (PBS) in the United States, which pioneered in techniques for the blind and hearing-impaired to use TV. The "vertical blanking interval" (VBI), the top twenty-one lines of a TV picture, can be used to transmit educational material at the same time as a regular broadcast. Each VBI line can transmit about twenty-nine pages of text or educational materials to schools, including teaching guides, student workbooks, computer software, bibliographies, research findings, and other materials needed by a student for a course. PBS has suggested that such materials, sent via VBI, could also be used by faculty to update their current teaching resources.

Nelson Heller (1991e) reports that the state of Maryland, seeking a relatively inexpensive way to send software and other course material to classroom instructors, tried piggybacking data transmission on a stereo audio subchannel of the state's public broadcasting TV system. It was found, however, that because programs for the hearing-impaired were located there, it was better to use the VBI for distance learning and cable-delivered programs. The reception equipment (for sending directly to computers or printers as well as TV sets) did not cost a school more than $500, and the course material could be then "filed" for repeated classroom use. This system is very cost-effective since it uses satellites and the ordinary TV equipment available in most communities.

THE GLOBAL MATRIX OF COMPUTER NETWORKS

Another large and comprehensive system at the heart of the emerging university is what John Quarterman (1990) calls "the Matrix," the interconnection of computer networks that has almost astonishing implications for university teaching and research as well as for students at all levels of learning. It takes Quarterman more than 700 pages to catalog and describe "the Matrix," so we include only brief illustrations here.

The National Science Foundation Computer Network for Research and Education (NSFNET) illustrates in America today what will soon be possible in the rest of the world. No one university, phone company, or corporation could alone do what was accomplished together by these three: IBM (which provided the design development and national "data highway"); the cooperating universities; and the MCI telephone system's extensive fiber optic and digital radio network. NSFNET provides the "backbone" that connects area computer network systems that link to Europe, Asia, and Latin America (IBM 1990). Many academic people and researchers connect to it through Internet.

Quarterman describes Internet as a worldwide network that actually interconnects many different kinds of educational and research networks. Not to be connected with it begins to limit scholars much as they are limited if they do not have access to the journals that report the latest research in their fields. Internet, which supports high speeds and powerful services, remains the most important computer network in the educational community (Arms 1990) until the completion of the high-speed optical fiber National Research and Education Network (NREN). Internet connects with NSFNET, EASInet (the European Academic and Research Community), and similar networks in other countries. Just as anyone with a telephone can dial any other phone no matter which telephone companies own the lines, so also a computer through Internet can connect with any other computer on the system. (PSInet, for a monthly fee, will connect anyone to Internet.)

Internet is a kind of cooperative, involving educational institutions, private corporations, and government agencies as well as individual researchers and their professional groupings. Those not involved have probably seen an Internet address (for the Internet Society: "isoc@nri.reston.va.us") without realizing it is more logical than a telephone number that one can use for a similar connection. Internet has several million users in twenty-six countries, inasmuch as many of its 5,000 connected networks are themselves very large (Cerf 1991). Its many component networks are funded differently, but largely from government grants and universities. Some governments are beginning to see these "electronic highways" as becoming to our global society what paved roads were for the Roman empire.

BITNET is a computer network that is less powerful, less expensive, and much less reliable, but one that reaches many smaller colleges that have not been able to afford the equipment and staff necessary for Internet. Set up by a consortium of universities in the United States, BITNET increasingly has connections (some of them not entirely legal) in universities on many continents. It is less reliable because messages are transmitted from computer to computer in a hodgepodge of connections across the country and the world.

Two of the crucial aspects of this computer networking technology are *gateways*, connections making it possible for a subscriber to one computer network to get in touch with someone on another, and efforts to expand free and low-cost services. This may involve using packet radio where telephone services are limited (see Quarterman 1990 on mobile vans for sharing transmission and reception costs).

THE LESS VISIBLE ACADEMIC CONNECTIONS

David Hughes and other pioneers in the Electronic Networking Association maintain that there is a third kind of connection that is overlooked in the shadow of satellite TV and the established computer networks. Some courses are offered and students in various countries are interconnected via this alternate system, for example, FidoNet for IBM computer users and FredNet for Apple computer users. These are more free-wheeling, amateur-type systems where on-line learning is generally self-directed, as when learners go on-line to ask where to get what they need to know.

This kind of system is most visible on tens of thousands of computer bulletin boards where a vast amount of learning and instruction takes place. While significant research is often coordinated in this way, most of the learning is not the kind a university generally recognizes as important. Yet independent, self-directed study is probably the wave of the future and pioneering on FidoNet, in telephone calls from one computer to another, or from a learner to a computer bulletin board, may prove to be tremendously important to the emerging worldwide electronic university.

It is not true that all less-advantaged countries lack access to electronic highways. Think what a powerful instrument the telephone is, interconnecting a hundred million phones via space satellites (and via cellular wireless phones [see Andrews 1991] and packet radio where there are not yet telephone lines). Also radio and television—and the Cable News Network—are everywhere, managed by interconnected computers. This global communications system is now becoming more and more two-way, through television "dish" receptors, videotape recorders, fax and packet radio, and empowering computer connections and software.

Until recently, computer-to-computer connections via ordinary telephone lines and satellite were often unreliable. A message sent from New York got to Shanghai in perfect shape, and then was jumbled over an antique phone line to a Shanghai office or home. Now, however, very fast modems (to connect telephone and computer) include effective error-correcting technology that reduces that unreliability so that increasingly it is less a problem for educational connections. Recently also, the major manufacturers of the modems that connect computers and telephones have agreed on common standards. And students in China and elsewhere are learning simple, inexpensive, and remarkably imaginative ways to improvise computer/telephone connections with a pair of pliers, sending overseas for $3 a long document that otherwise would cost $300 to transmit (Hughes 1991).

UN PROPOSAL FOR LATIN AMERICA

At the request of the government of Brazil, a United Nations Development Program (UNDP) report (Pugliatti 1989) prepared a plan for possible low-cost technology for higher education exchange in Latin America, a system that could be more people oriented than institution oriented. The proposal was introduced at a Latin American Networking Workshop held in Costa Rica in June 1989.

In order for a student or faculty member to participate in overseas course exchange, there were minimum needs that should be met.

First, users should have a type of *personal computer* that is available almost anywhere in the world (proposed: the Intel 80386 processor) and/or a satellite TV receiving dish.

Second, users should also have a *modem* to connect the computer to a telephone for electronic mail (E-mail), computer conferencing, and access to on-line bulletin boards and data base services. Much more important for research than a campus postboard in a hall, a bulletin board on a computer network allows users to post messages and replies at any time. It can be private or available to as many as tens of thousands of persons. Anyone with a computer and modem, for example, can connect free of charge to a "Disaster Information Center" bulletin board (information about hurricanes among other things) of Volunteers in Technical Assistance (VITA) via a telephone number available to the public. An on-line tutorial explains how to use the system (see "Bulletin Boards on the Internet," Marraccini 1991).

Third, the report suggested that Latin American universities need to connect to an adequate *computer conferencing system* with access to overseas data bases and research libraries. The existing and less expensive computer network proposed for initial use in Latin America is a portable version of the EcoNet/PeaceNet computer network system. It has been more widely available in Latin America than other systems and was suggested for use in conducting technical demonstrations in three countries that at that time were not well served by packet-switching networks. The purposes of this testing were to introduce local institutions to the technology; to develop relationships necessary for the establishment of permanent facilities; and to allow on-site testing of the system under rigorous conditions. It was proposed that the UNIX-based software and super-microcomputer hardware configuration presently used would be converted to run on a more portable computer system (Pugliatti 1989). Computer conferencing with such a system makes it possible for a college class to meet on-line. Users in different countries can interconnect regularly for personal or group conferences, which can be public, open to all, or private, limited to students registered for a class. The recommended Association for Progressive Communications (APC) software system enables this to happen through public data networks, local or long distance telephone, or radio.

Fourth, Latin Americans also need *affordable software* to operate the system, such as that offered free of charge—to nonprofit organizations— by the Institute for Global Communications and Community Data Processing. That APC system, recommended for Latin America, had the essential features of expensive computer-messaging systems now in use in industrialized countries, but was designed to be low cost and to use standardized, mass-produced equipment. Instead of requiring a big expensive mainframe computer, it had a distributed system interconnecting many small personal computers. One microcomputer system can therefore serve an area with up to 3,000 users, yet each system can easily be expanded as these small computers interconnect with other systems to link regions together. This greatly reduces the high cost of international computer networking and communications that interconnect via systems in the United States or Europe. Think how expensive long-distance phone calls would be, for example, if all calls had to be routed through a "switchboard" in London or Tokyo (although George Gilder [1990] says this soon may change in the more sophisticated communications systems). The APC provides local "switchboards" in Latin America, so computer conferencing need not go through London or New York. Local messaging networks can thus bypass expensive international systems. Users pay only for a local call but can still address their mail internationally. The GLOSAS/Global University project and cooperating university computer networking groups in South and Central America have been developing ways to drastically reduce telephone and television costs involved in educational exchange from country to country. Long-distance telephone costs *within one country* are often manageable, whereas *international* rates are often prohibitively high as set by government Post, Telegraph, Telephone (PTT) monopolies (for example, over

$350 an hour from Senegal to Europe). On the other hand, if all transmissions planned to and from, say, Bolivia in one day were combined and compressed, they could be sent overseas at very low cost. A local messaging system collects the international "mail" each day and compresses it, combining it with all other data to be sent that day, then sends it to the appropriate foreign connections in the middle of the night at a very high speed. Only a few minutes of telephone time are needed for an entire day's international communications. Furthermore, such compressed messages are automatically sent via the least expensive routes.

Meanwhile, the recommended APC system is easy to use and can be individually tailored to serve the specific interests and needs of its users, including "different language capabilities." This system, Enzo Pugliatti (1989) says, has operated in Nicaragua and in 1989 was being installed in Brazil.

Fifth, computer networking/conferencing can be supplemented with *fax machines*, which are widely used in Latin America to send pictures and documents. Term papers and exams from distance students can be sent quickly via telephone.

Sixth, cost reductions can be accomplished by use of *packet radio* where adequate phone service is lacking, and by use of a low earth-orbiting satellite for communications—that is, a smaller satellite that orbits nearer to the earth, such as the one sent up in 1984 by VITA, the University of Surrey in England, and the (HAM) Radio Amateur Satellite Corporation (Garriott 1990; Callihan 1989). It had on board "special transmitters and receivers that will operate in both amateur radio bands and experimental frequencies for which VITA has been licensed." It links radio and microcomputers, using the satellite to extend radio's transmission range. The ground stations are packet radios that send digital computer messages without telephones. (For technical detail, see the *Handbook* of the Amateur Radio Relay League or Quarterman 1990). PRNET is an experimental packet radio network that has been experimenting with the protocols and technology and with a connection to Internet. By 1985, John Quarterman reports, there were about 30,000 HAM radio amateurs with the capability of connecting with computer networks.

Seventh, Latin American users need a simple *gateways* system to connect with the principal commercial *E-mail* services, as well as with telex and fax; with virtually all of the noncommercial computer networks (free of charge), such as BITNET, which interconnects North American universities; and with computer conferencing systems to connect members of a class with the instructor. Through connections with similar networks existing in the United States, Canada, and Europe, and underway in Southeast Asia, India, Scandinavia, and Australia, the recommended APC system will enable worldwide communication and collaboration for Latin Americans. For locations not served by telephone, Latin American students and faculty can also exchange materials through UHF television-band broadcasts.

These proposals for Latin America tend to assume that most country-to-country connections will be class-to-class, or to provide special lectures or resources for a college course. The system may be used primarily by faculty and graduate students who need access to more up-to-date information than is available locally. Latin America may not for some time have many individual students connecting for self-directed study to another country.

Enzo Pugliatti points out that initial experimentation should demonstrate the possibilities of this proposed technology to governments and educational institutions; test the technology and the use of distributed network resources, for example, in countries like Brazil that are geographically extended; and seek to discover the legal, financial, technical, and institutional constraints to the establishment of a permanent network in each area, asking such questions as What technology is the most appropriate to the local situation? Are local organizations able and willing to operate the permanent system? Is it cost-effective? How much can Internet work costs be reduced, and how does this affect the economics of operating a node? How can user's cost be reduced? What system provides the best capability for keeping in close contact with students and tracking their progress?

The same questions, of course, should also be asked of the most sophisticated technological systems that are now increasingly available in Europe, America, and East Asia.

THE PACIFIC RIM: MORE SOPHISTICATED TECHNOLOGY

Joseph Pelton, formerly of INTELSAT and in 1991 director of the Interdisciplinary Telecommunications Program at the University of Colorado, outlined new technological possibilities in his address prepared for the November 1990 conference of the International Council of Distance Education in Venezuela. Options include, he said, one-way video plus audio return, one-way video with satellite as a videocassette distribution system, new kinds of earth station antennae, and videodiscs working together with personal computers and robotic devices.

Pelton has also pointed out that all the necessary hardware has been invented, that global electronic education's next priorities must be more sophisticated software. One example is the "virtual classroom" technology that was used by the ConnectEd program (New School for Social Research) for courses conducted on the Electronic Information Exchange System (EIES) computer network with instructors in North America and students in Asia, Europe, and Latin America (see Levinson in Mason and Kay 1989). Based at the New Jersey Institute of Technology, EIES and the "virtual classroom" (trademarked) were used by paying a monthly fee much like a telephone bill. Using it to take a class, a student in Asia dialed a local telephone number to connect to the mainframe computer in New Jersey in order to receive any course material stored there, to leave or receive papers, or to communicate with an instructor or other class members (see chapter 9 on types of "electronic class-rooms").

New kinds and combinations of technologies for communication in education are being experimented with and developed each day and each "new mix" brings the reality of the worldwide electronic university closer. For example, the GLOSAS/GU project is much interested in the Multi-Program TV (MPTV) as developed by the Broadcasting Science Research Institute, Ministry of Radio, Film and TV in China and the Science and Technical Research Laboratories of the Japan Broadcasting Corporation (NHK). This system can broadcast as many as forty-four different TV courses simultaneously on one channel, using Japan's BS–1 broadcasting satellite or China's communications satellite. Remote students can view a full-color, freeze-frame image with full audio annotation, "thus greatly reducing the satellite usage costs" (Utsumi 1989). Ordinary TV broadcasts twenty-five to thirty frames a second, many of them much the same. MPTV selects many fewer frames for transmission, cutting the broadcast time needed, for example, by sending only every other frame; at the receiving end the system then reproduces as many of the frames as needed. "The sound is also coded and is sent out alternatively with the picture signal."

INTEGRATED SERVICES DIGITAL NETWORK (ISDN)

"One innovation now being implemented on a global scale can aid tele-education to be lower in cost, to be more geographically extensive, and ultimately to be more powerful in educational applications" (Pelton 1990). The ISDN, Pelton says, provides the "electronic digital highway of tomorrow" that will have "universally accessible ports at any place, at any time." This will make an enormous contribution to the creation of global education networks. It is crucial, however, that a hundred nations involved in terrestrial and satellite networks use the same ISDN standards so that fiber optic cables and satellite networks can be inter-connected. Many more educational possibilities will open up when a thousand TV channels are available to the user.

Communicating on light beams—lightware communications net-works—involves more than the expanded possibilities of optical fibers for telephone and cable TV. Because there is no atmosphere, a satellite over the United States can form an optical link with another satellite over India. Global electronic education, Pelton says, will be totally digital. It would take twenty seconds to transmit the entire Library of Congress with high quality sound and graphics. A vast number of courses and lectures can be sent that quickly when lightware communications are combined with "digitally compressed two-way video," which by 1989 was already in use to connect dozens of campuses.

Another emerging technology that can empower worldwide electronic courses is simultaneous language translation software (Wood 1989). As automatic computer translation matures, whether in the form of automatic subtitles appearing on a TV screen or a computer voice that automatically translates from English to Japanese, it will link the world's scholars and universities as never before.

It is hard to predict what technologies will be used in education in the future "because the technology is changing every 18 months" (Lewis 1991). Greg Kearsley (1985) suggests that international business corporations will continue to pioneer in developing new technologies that will then be used by education. Joseph Pelton (1990), after using a chart to compare merits of various systems, concludes that fiber optic educational networks are well suited for educational piggybacking on top of public telecommunications systems at modest cost. The best educational networks, he says, will be hybrid in nature. "In rural areas VHF terrestrial radio links may feed to satellite terminals that in turn may link to fiber optic cable networks which then extend to urban production centers." And Pelton is encouraged that "reduced costs will make a cornucopia of educational services available to more and more people on a global basis."

The next chapter reports on the use of new communications technologies for global-scale research projects. (For more detail on the technology that is still written in clear language for the lay reader, see Cerf 1991 and other articles in the September 1991 issue of *Scientific American*.)

Five

INTERNATIONAL RESEARCH TEAMWORK

The most important aspect of this new information technology environment is the capability it provides for ... collaboration ... [and] those interactions will be among people from an incredible variety of cultural backgrounds ... from many different nations.

Douglas Van Houweling 1991

The worldwide electronic university can already be seen in the research projects of scholars in many countries who are linked together electronically, working together as if they were in the same laboratory. Global co-laboratories, using computer networks and next-to-lightning-fast optical networks, can increasingly mobilize many minds and thus facilitate a collective intelligence that may turn out to be at least as significant as artificial intelligence.

Interlocking networks of scholars from many colleges who work in the same fields of research often have greater loyalty to their discipline, and to the associations of scientists in the same field, than they do to the university that employs them. In that sense, that is, through their professional associations, international scholarly journals, and conferences of philosophers or biologists, they were already part of an invisible worldwide university before it had any electronic dimension.

Global-scale research tools and interconnected computer technology first has empowered researchers to work together internationally in science, in medicine, in space exploration and related astronomy research as well as in international earthquake and weather projects. Huge simulations of the world's economy and earth observation satellites are illustrations of global-scale instruments.

NSFNET AS TOOL

The National Research and Education Network (NREN), which represents a highly significant investment for research, will be built on the foundation laid by the National Science Foundation Computer Network for Research and Education (NSFNET). "NSFNET proves that government, higher education, and business and industry can work together effectively to serve the research and education community" (IBM 1990). With gigabite transmission speeds, NSFNET is "bringing the world of ideas together," linking over a thousand research centers (university, business, and government). It enables hundreds of thousands of researchers to access supercomputing centers, library and satellite data, medical images, scientific instruments (at a far distance), and other high-technology equipment. It provides the "backbone" and hubs to link other networks, including research networks in Canada, Europe, Latin America, and the Pacific Rim (see Smith 1991). It has been compared to America's network of highways that enables travelers to go wherever and whenever they wish, rather than being tied to train or plane schedules. Using it, "collaborations among distant colleagues are creating invisible colleges, institutions without walls, and co-laboratories" (IBM 1990). "Global-scale tool" seems too small a word to apply to this powerful combination of computer networks.

THE CO-LABORATORY

William Wulf and Laurence Rosenberg (1990) use the spelling "collaboratory" for the interaction of scholars "with instrumentation, with data, with journals and books, but most importantly with each other." It is not a place, they say, but an electronic environment; it has "all it takes to support ... productive collaboration." They propose as collaboratory models:

- experimental multimedia conferencing systems, such as the "Information Science Institute system," that "support video and audio transmission, and document authoring and commenting among multiple sites";
- the Internet computer network for researchers that supports access to distributed data bases;

- the system that enables astronomical objects to be remotely accessed internationally;
- the biology community's data bases on the genome of some organisms;
- and instruments in space and under the ocean that can be remotely controlled by scientists from different locations.

They note that a co-laboratory encourages interdisciplinary cooperation among scholars who are located on different campuses, and can make it possible for homebound persons, such as those with disabilities, to participate.

Not only do scholars thus work together regularly on an international scale as never before, but they can now create tools to deal with kinds of problems that previously have been too complex and difficult. Across the centuries, whenever scholars have contemplated overwhelming complexity, they have been tempted by two alternatives: to despair or to oversimplify through specialization and exclusion. The latter alternative has sometimes led to a loss of truth, to manipulation and abuse of knowledge, and at best to overspecialization, which has lost sight of the whole picture.

By contrast, computers and international computer networks are now enabling researchers to do their work faster, more efficiently, more creatively, more comprehensively, and more collaboratively; as a result, the ever-growing need for holistic approaches to global projects is now more obtainable. Computer-managed intellectual tools such as "groupware" and BITNET, as well as successor computer networks that increasingly will interconnect all the world's universities, can do more than empower individual minds to undertake projects of greater depth and scope. They now transcend geography, as computer networking is making it possible for scholars scattered over the earth to work together daily, transcending limits of time and place.

THE HUMANITIES ALSO

Scholarly electronic interconnections now influence research in the humanities as well as in the sciences. Willard McCarty, for instance, at the 1990 Association for Information Science (ASIS) annual assembly reported on his three-year experience (1987–89) as editor of "Humanist," an on-line computer conference. He and other panelists at a session on "Telecommunications and the Humanities" reported highly significant research cooperation. Perhaps it is too early, he said, to evaluate procedures that are hardly twenty years old when the technology is changing so fast and where an adequate vocabulary does not as yet exist. Just as the automobile was first called a "horseless carriage," so the term "computer bulletin board" suggests something marginal and casual in higher education and thus prejudices some scholars who might coordinate research through such international computer and telecommunication means.

McCarty also pointed out that most scholars are not yet clear about what the function of such telecommunications may be in research. A limited and prejudicial vocabulary speaks of "electronic journals" (see Wilson 1991). Actually, the fluid text on-line may never replace the printed journal—used in establishing credentials or for faculty evaluation in advancement of promotion—as the final and permanent record. The computer conference and on-line publications, rather, are a way to test ideas, to carry on dialog each day—or whenever one wishes—with other scholars as can be done at professional meetings (see McDonald 1991).

Humanities scholars on various continents, who may rarely or never see each other in person, can create an ongoing "community of scholars" who meet on-line as often as they wish, each at his or her own convenience, to report, discuss, argue, debate, refine, help each other, and develop joint research. Such "electronically connected" research groups can do more and more together as the technology matures and scholars have more experience with it.

Also described at the 1990 ASIS conference was COM-SERVE, an on-line forum and service for over 15,000 students and professors. The service, with computer facilities provided by Rensselaer Polytechnic Institute, with the work done largely by volunteers, has been entirely free. Where McCarty's "Humanist" was a one-person volunteer project, operated from his home on a personal computer, the university-funded COM-SERVE provides a large variety of services and takes pride in doing so in a style that is easy for any first-time user:

- on-line data bases, 1500 files with ninety bibliographies related to the professional field;
- pedagogical material including syllabi, exams, and model materials to improve quality of work;
- a directory of scholars, complete with areas of expertise and specialized research, with instruction on how to contact them on-line or via the post office or telephone (note also: a data base of research in progress reported by Richards 1990);
- a directory of funding sources for research projects, of job openings, conferences, and graduate school programs and curricula;
- an on-line index to scholarly journals in the field, accessible by author, subject, title, or words in title;
- a "hot line" for asking questions, and for groups to "get together" for discussion, casual explorations, or to coordinate serious research (about one third of participation is for serious ongoing work, and the rest is less formal discussion about subjects of concern, explorations, and queries);

- a "file" where papers can be placed to invite comment on them;
- a "news file" to report recent developments in the field of research;
- an index;
- and varied "support services" from which a participant who has any kind of problem with the technology or procedures can ask questions and get help.

This kind of project makes it possible to eliminate much wasteful duplication of research and can regularly and inexpensively connect a scholar—often the only one on a campus working on a particular type of research area—with others who share the same interest even if they are on the other side of the world.

A study by the Institute for Scientific Investigation (Begley 1991) found that 45 percent of the 4,500 "supposed top-quality papers" from 74,000 science journals were not cited during the five years following publication. The implication is that nearly half of the scientific papers in the United States are "basically worthless." This suggests a great need for better coordination to reduce duplication and where possible to improve "petty projects" that are not of use to other scholars in society.

Increasingly useful on Internet (Marracini 1991) are computer bulletin boards that enable scholars to interconnect simultaneously when working on the same research project and also serve as a place to record the status and progress of joint work. Any participant on a different continent from colleagues can check the bulletin board at any hour of day or night, leaving or receiving information.

GRAND RESEARCH DESIGNS

The world is now confronted with many serious problems that can be solved only on a global basis. Examples are pollution of air and water, soil degradation, deforestation, the greenhouse effect, acid rain, and pollution, which spreads across national boundaries and threatens the ozone layer itself. It is paradoxical that so much scholarly work fails to be global because nationalism has a firm grip on universities. Faculty members so often forget that they are members of a cosmopolitan community. If universities are not to be intellectual ghettos, then the worldwide exchange of ideas and research is a necessity. This is true not only in science, but also in schools of business that in America still often focus narrowly on the domestic market at a time when business is becoming far more international.

Large-scale collaborative research can involve more "grand designs," to use a phrase from Kenneth Underwood's comprehensive Danforth-funded research that provided for collecting and storing computer data in such a way that future generations can continue to enlarge it and build on it. Or perhaps more important is the way a group of biologists in several countries can design and carry out a joint research project across vast distances, dividing up parts of the job and keeping in constant touch with each other. (See the international BIOSIS data base, Arms 1990.) Documentation, including graphics, can be sent instantaneously anywhere, anytime (Schmidt 1989), making major contributions to global health through an early warning system for earthquakes and for viruses like flu epidemics and AIDS. Many kinds of software are emerging to make it easier and more effectively possible for widely scattered scholars to work collaboratively in groups (Turner 1988).

Existing technologies and more holistic explorations of various scenarios can be combined in solving global social problems. All kinds of possibilities can then be explored through computer simulations. Expertise in modeling and gaming can be interconnected with global systems to empower explorations of new international institutions or to remodel existing ones. New precision can come into the diagnosis of problems and the definition of issues and alternatives. Comprehensive data, often not adequately brought to bear in solving many kinds of problems, can be pulled together so that computer modeling can be used to help make important decisions. Manfred Kochen's (1989) proposals for the future of the Library of Congress pointed out that such new technologies provide "more options for enhancing the intellectual work that is increasingly vital for governance."

SOME CURRENT GLOBAL-SCALE RESEARCH PROJECTS

Rather than carry on a theoretical discussion of research projects that point to an emerging electronic "invisible research university", we can illustrate with a list of some important areas of joint research between scholars on at least two different continents, who collaborate and regularly work together via computer conferencing, computer bulletin boards, and/or teleconferencing.

Physics

More than two hundred physicists on three continents participated in large high-energy physics experiments based at the Fermi National Accelerator Laboratory. The scientists passed "prototype programs back and forth electronically" and shared data generated by the accelerator. Recalling a communication from a laboratory in Switzerland, one physicist said, "It was one of the transition moments of my life." He felt that his horizon had just doubled in size as a result of the Physics Community Network (PHYSNET), which includes High Energy Physics (HEPnet), the Space Physics Analysis Network (SPAN), the Radio Astronomy Observatory Network (NRAO), and others that interconnect many scientists in Europe and Japan and many of which can be accessed from other countries (Quarterman 1990).

In 1991 a researcher at the Parallel Computing Research Facility at the Australian National University, Canberra, for example, was doing research on Argonne National Laboratory's connection machine. There was in Australia no machine of that size and power, so he used Internet via satellite to connect with Palo Alto, California. Also, a University of Newcastle researcher in Australia was doing collaborative work "with MIT in NASA's crustal dynamics program," shipping a large amount of data back and forth electronically each week (Smith 1991).

Humanitarian Research

Private and government international agencies that seek to serve those suffering from hunger, personal handicaps, disease, poverty, war, and disaster have pioneered in the development of computer networks, such as PeaceNet, and the instantaneous low-cost exchange of data and documents via packet radio and low-earth orbiting satellite, such as the one operated by British HAM radio. Jerome Glenn of the United Nations University (1989) points out that electronic services like CARINET, an international computer network for developing nations, help small entrepreneurs and students as well as major organizations and governments. CARINET pools users' expertise in areas such as disaster relief and development projects (Quarterman 1990).

Health and Medicine Research

It would take an encyclopedia to describe the extent of international medical research projects. Here are some Third World examples: Jorge Litvak, M.D. (1986), as coordinator of the Adult Health Program of the Pan American Health Organization, has pointed out that the introduction of electronic networking within the Latin American Cancer Research project "has been an important step for medical research in Latin America"; Dr. Jose Dominguez of the Chilean Internet Center said that, at a time when the most crucial components of medical research were getting more and more difficult to reach, this has been the most important development he has witnessed.

The Online Mendelian Inheritance in Man (OMIM) Project based at Johns Hopkins University is available free around the world and in 1991 had 1,500 registered participants (Lucier 1990). There were, for example, 195 users at the National Institute of Genetics in Mishima, Japan. The last three editions of the reference work *The Mendelian Inheritance in Man* have been published entirely from a tape of a data base to which scientists in various countries contribute electronically. The need for international cooperation in keeping the data base current and maintaining its integrity is seen in the fact that information in the related Human Genome Project (HGM) doubles every year.

Space and Astronomy Research

An Internet coordinating committee to bring together agencies working in space, defense, science, energy, and health was created in 1987 (Quarterman 1990) to communicate with CERN (European Nuclear Research) and RARE (European Standards Research). In Britain, Starlink connects astronomers and has links to networks in other countries. Astronomers on several continents can function as if they were together on one campus when they use space-based astronomy equipment such as the Hubbell Telescope. When functioning properly, astronomers can direct the equipment from numerous locations by means of a sophisticated computer-communications network. The amount of astronomy data being collected by the space administration is so vast that it would be impossible even for international teams of scientists to cope with it without global-scale electronic collaboration. For example, "the Ames Research Center . . . provides open . . . access to . . . 16,000 photographs from the Voyager 1 and Voyager 2 Spacecraft" (Rickard 1991).

International Environmental Research

The National Oceanic and Atmospheric Administration (NOAA), international earthquake studies, and the Global Observing System of the World Weather Watch share weather information among more than 120 countries. NOAA's environmental data about "the oceans, earth, air, space and sun and their interactions [used] to describe and predict the state of the physical environment" (Elkington and Shockley 1988) are available to many development projects in the Third World. Kevin Sanders (1986) describes the French Systeme Probatoire d'Observation de la Terre (SPOT), a powerful tool for providing data for a wide variety of research projects. The Global Monitoring System of the United Nations Environmental Program facilitates joint international research in ecology and plans eventually to have Global Computer Resource Information Database (GRID) capability operating in every country. The European Network for Environmental Technology Transfer (NETT) shares knowledge on pollution control. The World Resources Institute reports that "the potential contribution of geographical information systems to environmental management and sustainable development in Third World countries is clearly very considerable" (Elkington and Shockley 1988).

Walter Roberts of the National Center for Atmospheric Research in

Boulder, Colorado, was one of the founders of the "Greenhouse-Glasnost Teleconference," which linked scientists in America and the Soviet Union by computer mail. Their teleconference grew out of on-line discussions of the Western Behavioral Sciences Institute and developed a hypothetical global-warming scenario for the year 2050. Assessment essays were prepared by Soviet and American participants.

Unidata, which supplies university researchers with atmospheric data "in near real time" (Domenici and Smith 1991), is managed by the University Corporation for Atmosphere Research in Boulder. Not only is information shared—and software downloaded via the NSFNET computer network—but instruments can be controlled remotely to make corrections, for example, to a satellite antenna at the University of Alaska.

Agriculture

The agriculture database of the National Agricultural Library (AGRI-COLA)—using CARINET, established in part by the Partnership for Productivity and the Agricultural Cooperative Development International—helps to enable cooperative agriculture research among scientists in various countries (Quarterman 1990). International collaborative research is illustrated by the NOAA locust warning project, designed especially to help African countries, and by coordinated forestry projects, essential to prevent flooding and other disasters for agriculture.

Energy Research

Examples of collaborative approaches to energy management are "the Integrated National Emergency Planning system" in Sri Lanka and the shared Landsat information on the location of oil resources. Quarterman (1990) also reports on the Magnetic Fusion Energy Network (MFEnet) designed to interconnect laboratories doing research on nuclear fusion, in 1990 reported as interconnecting only North America and Japan; and the Energy Science network (ESnet) for all of the United States Department of Energy research programs, which is developing links to Europe and Japan.

Political Science

"Gaming" is another form of collaboration among researchers from country to country; political science students in different countries, for example, are linked for role playing and simulating international crises from the University of Maryland (Kerwin 1989). Using an international diplomacy simulation game (ICONS) involving universities in twenty locations around the world, "peace gaming" can be used to explore alternatives to war, as demonstrated in the use of an MIT-created computer data base in the United Nations "Law of the Sea"negotiations (see Antrim c.1986). Just as the Pentagon can without risk try alternative battle strategies through simulations—the Navy has connected computers at four locations, for war games—so also scholars can simulate and try alternative strategies for the world court or the United Nations. Also in an effort to make UN research information more widely available, the UN has established on FidoNet a directory of data bases and a UN yearbook (Quarterman 1990).

Economics

At a conference on "managing complexity" at the Penta Hotel in New York City in July 1986, Takeshi Utsumi used a computer conferencing network and the sixth generation comprehensive FUGI model of all the world's economies, at Soka University in Japan, to link economists across the Pacific in a simulation of what would happen if Japan spent as much of its gross national product on defense as the United States has done. It took the comprehensive system three days to work out the implications for the economies of various nations, as prominent economists studied the graphically presented spreadsheet results (see Utsumi 1989; Utsumi, Mikes, and Rossman 1986) with evidence that the U.S. trade and budget deficits would significantly decrease within several years.

COLLECTIVE INTELLIGENCE

Perhaps the primary importance of mind-empowering computer tools for the electronic university lies not in machines that will think for scholars but in scholars using such tools to amplify "collective intelligence," bringing many minds together for more effective collaborative research. The university at its best has been not only a place where isolated or specialized individuals work, but has long involved collective intelligence, most often in our time seen in the discourse at professional meetings and through scholarly journals. The global enlargement and empowerment of this process, to make possible a quality of joint work and thought that has never before been realized, is an important aspect of the emerging invisible worldwide electronic university.

Richard Kirby has defined collective intelligence (Kirby and Rossman 1990) as "the science of computer research-in-community, collegial research in which participants organize their energies so as always to be more than the sum of their separate parts." It is seen in the fusing of expertise through networks of minds which can result as thousands of interconnected parallel computers help scholars work simultaneously on different aspects of the same problem or project.

Scholars have always built upon the work of countless others who have gone before them, known and unknown, debating their ideas with students and colleagues, testing and enlarging concepts as ideas and systems grew. Only in this century have scholars found it possible to meet frequently with others around the world, so that it has been productive for minds to come together in conferences, bringing the insights from many cultures to pool their ideas and rich traditions, challenging each other and often experiencing a synergy. Scholars at international research conferences are now discovering how to continue the dialogue via computer conferencing, supplementing, and enhancing those face-to-face conferencing efforts before, during, and after the experience. For example, Edward Feigenbaum and Pamela McCorduck (1984) reported on the "network adventure" of a group of Japanese scientists, an effort to fuse many kinds of expertise in a "group quest," creating a "network of minds" in an area where no one specialist is adequate to deal with the whole problem.

Douglas van Houweling, vice-provost of the University of Michigan, said at the 1989 UW annual meeting that electronically-empowered collaboration is now beginning to enable "bursts of creative interaction" across cultural and international boundaries. (See also Tessler 1991; Arms 1989, 1990; and Kingsbury 1990 who discusses the Collaboratory project of the National Science Foundation and research to expand international electronic mail to include graphics, formatted text, spreadsheets, voice, and video.)

The next chapter reports on another dimension of international research—the increasing connections among the world's research and university libraries.

Six

CONNECTING THE WORLD'S RESEARCH LIBRARIES

The universal electronic database may be individual or collective . . . vast . . . repositories of information available immediately to any user in the nation or world . . . millions of texts . . . to be managed and . . . joined to one world network.

Jay Bolter 1991

At the heart of traditional universities are great libraries, which Richard Dougherty (1991) says are at present not used by students and faculty as much as is commonly supposed. And one of the signs of the world-wide electronic university is an emerging global electronic research library system that is beginning to increase that use. It may sound like science fiction to talk yet about it, but what is first developing in North America, East Asia, and Europe can in time be extended to every continent: on-line access to all the world's important information by every scholar in the world. For some countries that may be a dream for a future century, but many students and faculty already participate in its beginnings.

A scholar's library in the early European universities consisted of his own personal collection of books or manuscripts. Then, as shared collections grew, the library evolved into a place, a building where scholars could rummage and explore books as they wished in a centralized book collection. The library later came to be seen as a staff of experts who could help the scholar obtain whatever was needed. And today a university library is less and less a place for books and printed materials alone; it also supplies the scholar with resource materials such as films, video- and audiocassettes, microfiche, tapes, CD-ROM and computer diskettes, and on-line data bases with interconnections that are increasingly international.

Many universities have merged their libraries and computer centers, and "library resources" are increasingly in hyperspace. The use of microcomputers and sophisticated telecommunications systems by faculty and students means that "service requirements in the electronic university will be driven and shaped by this increasing use of technology" (Arms 1990). "An unprecedented flexibility in the hands of the user to define and satisfy individual requirements" increasingly frees the scholar from the constraints of the traditional library.

Few people took it seriously four decades or so ago when Watson Davis, one of the founders of ASIS, predicted a global electronic library. Now, however, such a system is coming into existence, although different models for it exist in contemporary demonstrations and explorations. Kenneth King, formerly a provost at Cornell University and in 1991 president of EDUCOM says that the goal now is to create a world university network to connect every scholar with every important source of information—at no cost to the user—via an enabling "information management system" (Arms 1990).

Edwin Brownrigg (1990) points out that some fields of study, such as law, "have already created a kind of electronic library" and that we should be prepared for several different types to emerge. A "virtual library" will require bilateral and multilateral agreements to be negotiated on location of data, finances, and exchange standards, and on technologies that differ drastically from country to country. Nevertheless, a global electronic library is coming into existence in the form of interconnected networks linked to clusters and consortia of libraries of various kinds (see Bolter 1991).

A major step was the "linked systems project" to connect the network of libraries related to the Online Computer Library Center (OCLC), the Research Library Group, the Washington Library Network, and the Library of Congress (Lynch 1990). This project undertook a pioneering role in working on international standards and projects "that affected every library and university." The Library of Congress, Manfred Kochen has pointed out (1988), is at a turning point in its history: "the nerves of government are being augmented by the technologies of freedom." New technologies provide more options for amplifying the intellectual work that is so essential for information age governance. (It is now possible for distant users to access the electronic catalog of the Library of Congress.) Kochen's research at the Library of Congress on how to improve its functioning would transform it into a "referral and facilitation service" in a network of many libraries.

A campus electronic library is "not just a local collection of hardware and software with information stored electronically or optically" (Kibbey and Evans 1989). It is a *network* of information tools and services, which may be located in many different places, including connections to other continents. An electronic library makes it possible for scholars to have access to that information network no matter where they may be working. That library/network should in time provide full access to text and not just to bibliographical information; and the system will be easy to use without becoming a computer expert.

Those of us who are not library specialists can get a glimpse of some models of the future global electronic library by looking at "revolutionary changes"—as well as at overwhelming difficulties faced—in the library systems of major universities, as described, for example, in *Campus Strategies for Libraries and Electronic Information* (Arms 1990).

University libraries—and especially their computerized card catalogs—are becoming increasing interconnected and coordinated electronically. I can now sit at my computer terminal and read the electronic card catalog of several major university libraries. (*Boardwatch* magazine tells how; the HOLLIS system at Harvard University, for example, can be accessed via modem at 617–495–9500.)

Sometime in the next century the world's research libraries can be united in a comprehensive electronic index/catalog of all of their combined resources. All students and faculty members at all colleges and universities could then access this on-line catalog from any telephone, using a computer terminal at home or from dormitory rooms or faculty offices. This of course would be only the beginning; a library is much more than a catalog.

WHAT CAN A DEVELOPING COUNTRY'S UNIVERSITY AFFORD?

The president of a university in the Philippines, just completing a new library building, now wants to make that library a more adequate servant of students and faculty by exploring "possible connections to the world." Now is the time for such a university to develop a long-range electronic library plan, and to begin experimenting, even though funds are not yet available for what would be most advantageous. Such a plan might include:

- first, identifying and training library personnel who can now undertake experimentation;
- second, planning with a consortium of universities in the same city to

develop a long-range plan in which each university library would co-operatively undertake certain phases of a development in which all would share, for example, the possibility of the consortium, a sort of regional electronic library center serving several universities;

• third, seeking some modest grants for the experiments of this consortium; investigating the needs of local business that might be served on a pay-for-use basis;

• and, fourth, perhaps establishing a "sister library" relationship with a North American university (one with an on-line electronic catalog that could be accessed from the Philippines) to share some resources and on-line connections on an experimental basis.

A university in Southeast Asia would probably first want to provide research information (and interpretation of it) to faculty and graduate students on CD-ROM. The cooperative library consortium could also determine which are the most needed research areas—perhaps agriculture, engineering, and health—and seek some free experimental access time from such databases as the U.S. Agricultural Library and the Institutes of Health. This would help discover ways to reduce costs. A network might then be developed to connect all universities in the Philippines with some Pacific Rim electronics libraries, perhaps first of all in Japan, Taiwan, and Australia where an electronic library system for Southeast Asia has been under consideration.

EUROPE, JAPAN, AND NORTH AMERICA

One way to discover what is happening in the more developed countries is to describe electronic library use by Jane, an undergraduate student today. Before she came to Columbia University in New York City, she already had access to almost any book through interlibrary loan and a requested book might come to her from half a continent away. Such library services available to her at the university are greatly expanded because Columbia is committed to collaboration with other universities and information networks.

To be able to make use of such services, Jane has taken a course, "Research in the Humanities," to learn how to use a remote data base as well as nearby resources. During the 1990–91 school year, Columbia was installing a system whereby students and faculty can in their own offices or rooms access the electronic catalogs of many other universities, for example, the University of Colorado library and the archives system of the University of Minnesota library. Such services can next be extended to the world, for example, to the data base of Tamking University in Taiwan, which is part of the OCLC system.

In the 1960s the Ohio College Association initiated what became the

Online College Library Center (OCLC, Inc.) with headquarters near Columbus, Ohio. This center has become the world's largest "bibliographic computer system," (McGill and Racine in Arms 1990), including sound recordings, music scores, maps, journals, and audiovisual materials as well as books. By 1986, it was serving over 8,000 libraries *in twenty-six countries* including, for example, the data base of Kinki University library in Osaka, Japan. OCLC is committed by charter to "furthering the ease of access and use of the ever-expanding body of worldwide scientific, literary and educational information" (McGill and Racine in Arms 1990).

While electronic on-line access at present is largely to catalogs and abstracts, a photocopy of an article can be faxed to a computer in a distant city. In some universities a student in one library can now ask to see a page of text from another library on a computer terminal screen. Also Columbia University is developing a much more comprehensive and inexpensive system to make the full text of a book or journal article available on a TV-type screen. So if using fax is too expensive a way to secure information from an overseas library, a student can print out all or any part of the text she is reading on her computer screen.

The resources of a great library can be accessed by the distance student in two ways: via computer connections to full text data bases or via CD-ROM, which allows for instant word search and access. Sony Corporation is marketing a "juke box" that can play twenty optical discs for instant search and retrieval of information from the equivalent of 60,000 five-hundred-page books (Arms 1990). Another "juke box," Pioneer's LC–V330 multi-disc changer, holds up to seventy-two laser discs with the capability of handling more (Heller 1991e). As this technology becomes cheaper with mass production, libraries with limited funds can thus obtain access to all of the world's major scholarly encyclopedias and reference books, electronically updated on a regular basis. Meanwhile Columbia is proceeding to make it possible for such discs to be automatically searchable from any student's room or faculty office. If the book on disc is not available at Columbia, a scholar can be connected to a CD-ROM disc at another library.

A larger world of scholarship opens up to students with the help of Columbia's "Integrated Academic Management System" through the network of libraries that now is expanding around the world. Jay Bolter (1991) reports resulting transformations in the organizing and use of materials.

A historian was told that he would one day be able to request immediate access to and read—via a TV-style monitor at his home or office—a page from a manuscript from as distant a place as a Portuguese museum. He admitted that this could greatly facilitate research, but complained that "it would take all the fun out of the work. Rather than having a page from an ancient manuscript shown me on a computer terminal," he said, "I would more enjoy going to Portugal to rummage around in a musty old museum." Then he asked: "How many millions of students in the world could the museum accommodate even if they could afford to travel?"

ORGANIZED INFORMATION

As the information explosion continues and it becomes increasingly difficult to manage the vast amounts of information available, the emerging electronic library also seeks better ways to organize (see next chapter) and to make available this huge corpus of human knowledge. ASIS publications report many experiments and developments in electronic indexing, transmission, and coding of library materials. An enlarging network of information professionals, sometimes coordinated with each other and sometimes not even knowing about each other's research, are at work on the foundations for a worldwide electronic library, even before they see or know how their work will ultimately integrate the world's knowledge.

Eric Drexler (1987) points out that "a large, highly evolved hypertext system is already "on its way to becoming a world electronic library." Materials in digital form can be continually reorganized and indexed in all kinds of ways that can better facilitate study and use. A dedicated computerized/videodisc/hypermedia encyclopedia system, for example, can include all relevant materials on a particular subject. Where printed books and encyclopedias include photo illustrations, the hypermedia system already can also include moving picture illustrations, lab demonstrations, music, and graphics. One can ask the system to search for more detailed information or illustrations at any point, for it not only stores documents and visual materials, but also develops links between them, idea by idea. And more and more links are developed each time a scholar uses the system.

So, Drexler says, hypertext can represent human knowledge in a more natural way. "Human knowledge forms an unbroken web, and human problems sprawl across the fuzzy boundaries between fields." Rows of books, he says, do a poor job of representing these connections, the structure of human knowledge. Despite all the best efforts of librarians to create webs by indexing, "library research still daunts all but a dedicated minority of the reading public." This changes and improves in a hypertext-based electronic library system where ideas can be seen in their largest contexts and where what humanity does *not* know, the "holes in arguments," to use Drexler's phrase, can be more visible to potential researchers.

Some of the problems hypertext poses for libraries are discussed in

Caroline Arms' book (1990) but what libraries now begin to provide for resident students will next be available on-line for distance students. Using an on-line multimedia electronic encyclopedia, for example, they will be able to see history come alive with pictures that move. A student will be able to listen to a symphony while following the score on-line and while watching a film about the composer, once all the recorded knowledge of mankind—written, spoken, painted or performed—is fully indexed and cross-referenced in electronic and machine-searchable form (Stewart 1991). To cite one illustration from *ASIS SIGnews*, 1989: the Great Dictionary of the Yiddish Language includes 200 texts from every era and locality where Yiddish has been spoken and a "machine-readable entry file including citations, historical, etymological and dialectological information, as well as English and Hebrew glosses and explanations."

ACCESS TO DATA BASES

Others see the global electronic library as consisting of the computer-telematic interconnection of all the world's data bases, the incorporation of vast electronic data bases of information stored in various parts of the world. In 1989 more than 6,000 public data bases were increasingly accessible to libraries and thus became part of the global library system. Some of the commercial data bases most widely used by students are: the National Newspaper Index, the Applied Science and Technology Index, and the Social Sciences Index. Essential to these are the ease and speed with which they can be searched.

The U.S. government has many comprehensive data bases, at the Department of Agriculture and the National Institutes of Health, for instance. Under one proposal, such government information could be made available at minimal cost to any and all libraries that might wish to record sections on videotape. "Publication" of government reports and documents in cross-indexed and easily accessible form would be transmitted via TV and satellite in the middle of the night, and could thus be available to libraries free of charge. This kind of transmission could be financially very advantageous to Third World libraries and others with modest budgets.

So far, most scholarly information systems, such as the comprehensive pedagogical research (ERIC) system, provide only titles and abstracts but not full text. The scholar needs much more than the list of books and journal articles that result from an electronic catalog search. The Cornell University's "scholarly information project" (Arms 1990) is one of many efforts to make it possible for researchers to obtain an electronic copy of any document that may be needed. The full text of a document might be consulted on computer or TV screen (access by cable TV) and then could be printed out if it contained what is required. This implies a sophisticated electronic "work station" with a high-resolution monitor and management system software. After a period of demonstration and experimentation, Cornell's system intends to provide access to the entire AGRICOLA data base of the National Agricultural Library to scholars across electronic networks and also to the BIOSIS data base in genetics. The latter data base is already international (Arms 1990). Cornell's network has gateways to NSFNET and thus to scholars in many countries. (And, see Arms 1990 for other systems for making the full text of documents available electronically.)

THE ON-LINE REFERENCE LIBRARIAN

Not only are reference materials becoming available in new and more manageable form, but the tasks of reference librarians are also changing. One feature of the prototype "Mercury Electronic Library" at Carnegie Mellon University is to be an artificial-intelligence-controlled "reference assistant" to guide users through the electronic library and automatically connect them to the right data base. Many distant scholars, when in need of information that may not yet be in print or on-line, put a request on a computer bulletin board that can be read all over the world. The scientist in Berlin who asks the question may get answers from Australia and California. So one university library has assigned a reference librarian to regularly read as many scientific bulletin boards as possible so as to be informed on such up-to-date scientific information.

In Japan the idea of an electronic library of videodiscs on satellite has been seriously proposed and discussed. Anyone in even the most remote college in Asia or Africa could then use a modest-priced dish receptor to get access to a university library, which in time could be as comprehensive as the Library of Congress. And for important work, the latest information that is not yet on the videodisc or satellite could be accessed (using systems already in place for use by business and government) via computer network from on-line data bases that could be more and more frequently updated.

In February 1989 one plan for such a "Space Station Library System" was proposed by Takeshi Utsumi's GLOSAS project together with Global Education Associates. The proposal was a response to the interest of the Japanese government in launching a satellite for educational programs around the Pacific and to the idea of the president of Tufts University who advocated a three-satellite system to be used exclusively for academic purposes, which would cover the entire globe.

Arthur C. Clarke has demonstrated in Sri Lanka a combination of computers and a bank of videotape recorders to create and index a new kind of research library. In an address he gave at the University of

Moratuwa in Sri Lanka where he is chancellor, Clarke said that new instruments—sooner than educators expect—are going to empower scholars in the mountains of Asia and in the bush of Africa to do more than use the libraries of universities on other continents. Even the smallest and most remote school, even the most isolated researcher, will be able to gain access to information from satellites as business firms do. Any school can download from international TV to develop a large electronic taped library, built around research interests and needs and indexed according to research plans. (See Hezel 1991 on an Annenberg-funded project to help colleges enrich their resources by assessing remote libraries.)

COMPREHENSIVE ELECTRONIC FACILITIES

Now that libraries are seen less as brick and stone and more as electronic systems, some universities are developing new kinds of buildings as interconnected electronic research centers. Library facilities designed especially for electronic use and their interconnections can be specially designed to coordinate all kinds of equipment to meet widely varying needs. At its heart, however, the library will be a network "in which the books rearrange themselves at the reader's request" and browsing can be greatly facilitated when the same book reappears on many "shelves" under every subject to which it is related (Bolter 1991).

Many projects are underway that are not yet completely designed or funded but that point to the emerging shape of the global research library. In the spring of 1988, for example, Carnegie Mellon University and the OCLC announced a plan to build an electronic library that can bring to any scholar's desk all the information he needs for his research projects (Turner 1988b). At present only libraries can subscribe to the services of OCLC, which provides bibliographic services and a data base of over seventeen million records; the Carnegie Mellon plan will also serve the individual scholar.

The prototype library, called "Mercury," is to be "both a laboratory in which researchers will study how people use electronic information, and a working reference library" (Arms and Michalak in Arms 1990). One purpose will be to demonstrate what an electronic library can do and become; another aim will be to serve as a working library to research costs and issues of copyright and intellectual property protection. As the American Association for Artificial Intelligence has already agreed to do, the directors of this project hope to persuade publishers, for example, of scholarly books, to provide their materials to the library in electronic form. Each new electronic journal or book can then easily be integrated into the existing system for search and indexing. The next task then will be to find ways to create on-line library systems that will provide researchers with easy ways to get the information they need and "to shift from one electronic source to another [as they] follow a train of thought." The speed of such a system can make it financially advantageous to distant students.

Dana Scott, a member of the Mercury Planning team, is quoted (in Arms 1990) as saying that the computerized library will also be able to solve problems created by printed materials. Not only will access be easier, with electronic means for pursuing a topic through a large corpus of materials, but electronic information can be more comprehensive. For example, an electronic dictionary can have levels of information, "starting with definitions, and going on to etymology, dialect forms, usage notes, synonyms, and cross references [bringing] back more concern about completeness of definitions . . . at several levels of detail, not all of which have to be visible at one time." In other words, limits of space on the page and space in a building need no longer constrain the expansion of information. There can be footnotes to footnotes to footnotes.

SOME PROBLEMS TO BE SOLVED

Any international system inevitably runs into road blocks. Some of the problems involved in creating a global library and electronic university system are political. These barriers can often be gradually eliminated when possibilities are demonstrated and ways are found to fund the system.

Costs of Books

With inflation continuing to increase the cost of printed materials, and with the costs of labor and paper accelerating, even poor schools will by necessity increasingly turn to electronic materials. A panel of publishers reported that the book that used to cost $3 now costs $30 and will in the future cost $300. By that time the same information on disk which used to cost $300 and now costs $30 will then cost $3. Furthermore, electronic books will not as often be discarded but can be updated from year to year for use by the next generation of students. Such electronic materials, easily connected with library systems, can provide ease and efficiency in scholarly work and when text on paper is desired it can be printed out.

Free Access?

As society moves into an information-age "learning society" with huge numbers of research scholars, and with all educated people doing some serious research from time to time, society probably cannot or will not in many countries afford to provide unlimited free time for everyone to use many of these electronic global library services. University tuition charges will provide for a certain amount of free time (more for graduate students) and public libraries will perhaps provide some free time for each borrower as an expansion of the interlibrary loan system. Beyond that, there probably will be charges for continued use of out-of-town data bases (not charges for using local CD-ROMs). Many people worry that the free library concept will be lost and the global electronic system will be available only to an elite. Of course, anyone who has asked the price (for a nonstudent) of a library card at an Ivy League college will see that many of the best libraries are already available only to an elite. The global electronic system can therefore be a considerable improvement over the present. Also, since the world's economy cannot thrive until a much higher percentage of the world's population has access to better information, there is incentive to provide better library resources for all.

Disappearing Information?

Richard Pierce (1990) points out that electronic technology "creates a cultural filter" and what does not pass through this filter may be neglected or lost. So who is to control the filter and decide what is to be included? Eric Drexler (1987) worries that electronic books will be erased, as print files and old books are also thrown away. Who is developing long-range policy on what is to be preserved electronically in libraries?

Monopoly Control?

Judith Turner (1990a) asks whether government or commercial data bases will in the future control information. Librarians, she says, "would rather let countries on the Pacific Rim control online information in the U.S. than leave it to the publishing industry." A survey of librarians found that they hope universities will control the information, perhaps forty leading universities creating "the largest online information repository in the world." Their second choice would be a $5 billion online library that would start with and build upon the Library of Congress. Less popular alternatives would be a rather chaotic segmented system with no standards, a consortium of Asian governments moving into the vacuum, or a worldwide consortium of publishers who establish a worldwide network.

Overload

The University of Illinois subscribes to more than 94,000 printed journals (Arms 1990). There is considerable debate over whether this kind of mushrooming scientific information can and should be provided electronically to save space and funds and to make it more easily searchable (Watkins 1991). Some faculty and library staff get nostalgic for the old ways; others are frustrated by the sophisticated technology involved in the electronic library. Perhaps the most important funding question is when and how adequate and affordable software will be developed to transcend such difficulties.

On-line Library Help to Distant Students?

Perhaps a more crucial question for the student in Africa who is electronically connected to the library in Asia is how to get the personal help which the staff of an on-campus library provides. To serve the distant student, the research/teaching library changes from one that conserves knowledge to one that distributes knowledge, one that can keep up with the rapid increase in knowledge and help scattered students cope with it. The electronic "high-tech" library that can show the distant agricultural student films that demonstrate new methods of water conservation, for example, may better serve him than does the book that he has on his desk. (On other issues, see Arms 1990.)

The next chapter is about the role of universities in organizing the world's knowledge electronically.

Seven

THE EMERGING GLOBAL ENCYCLOPEDIA AND WORLD BRAIN

> ... a tremendous hypertext encyclopedia [within which] every expert in every field maintains his or her knowledge online. Such a document can only keep growing and assimilating more and more information.
>
> Luke Young et al., 1988

An often overlooked dimension of the emerging electronic university is the comprehensive organization of all knowledge, as proposed in the World Brain idea of H. G. Wells. Perhaps the term is an unfortunate one, but Wells was prophetic—writing long before computers and online data bases—in predicting an encyclopedic worldwide coordination of knowledge that would be "alive and growing, changing continually ... every university and research institution feeding it ... every fresh mind brought into contact with it ... its contents the source of the instructional side of school and college work" (Wells 1938). (Many of the works cited in this chapter can be found in the World Brain Bibliography section of the Bibliography at the end of this book.)

Wells called for a "universal organization and clarification of knowledge and a closer synthesis of university and educational activities ... operating by an enhanced educational system through the whole body of mankind." He saw this as involving also a coordination of universities and research institutions, which we now see in the emerging worldwide electronic university. He spoke of the enormous waste involved in the duplication of uncoordinated research and foresaw a renaissance and renewal of humanity—or more than education alone—through and along with the development of a continually enlarging "world encyclopedia."

Wells proposed that the universities would be the place of verification, of continual testing and revising. "Thus every conflicting system of thought, idea, theory . . . would be brought into continuing dialog with every other." So the world encyclopedia would become, he thought, a World Brain in that it "will be much more than an assembly of fact." It will be "an organ of adjustment, adjudication, a clearing house of mis-understandings," an instrument for synthesis, a filter, a place to coor-dinate all research, a global network of intelligent workers and researchers, in other words, a super-university.

In addition to Wells, another historic document often cited as impor-tant in the beginnings of the World Brain concept is Vannevar Bush's "As We May Think" (1945), in which he proposed a system to deal with the growing complexity of human knowledge.

UNDERSTANDINGS OF THE WORLD BRAIN?

Terms such as world mind, World Brain, and global encyclopedia can suggest connotations that are not acceptable to many. Professor Glynn Harmon of the University of Texas once reported, tongue in cheek, that a NASA employee felt that the term World Brain was too limited and narrow. Why not "interstellar brain?"

Although the following list suggests that the terms mean different things to different people, there is in fact a considerable consensus con-cerning the meaning of World Brain among those who have given serious thought to it. Some of the differences may indicate chronological stages of development, yet each of these dimensions (*collection of knowledge, coordination of knowledge, integration/synthesis, and accessibility,* a concern since John Amos Comenius [1657]) has a developmental history of its own.

In the World Brain literature we find World Brain described as follows:

A collection of knowledge. Today, for example, it may be seen as an electronic interconnection of all the *world's libraries and data bases* (ASIS discussion reported by Andel 1987). The World Brain is thus seen as an interconnection of libraries and data bases of government and the United Nations, academia, and business corporations.

Schemes for coordinating all the world's knowledge. (See Nelson 1987, for example, on the Autodesk Company's software for a universal library system to cross-index and link all human knowledge.) There are many such proposals, such as REGISTER III, an effort of Professor H.J.A.

Goodman (1974) of the University of Calgary to combine his ideas with a composite of the many organizational schemes put forward at that time. Dr. James Grier Miller (in 1991 chairman of the board of the UW project) in the early 1960s proposed to establish a community of scholars who would work on general systems theory with the aim of integrating knowledge (Gordon, Blair, and Lindsay 1989).

Also, Manfred Kochen has elaborated Wells' idea of "a board of editors who would screen, sift, commission works of synthesis, and organize all the world's knowledge . . . so as to reflect, in coherent, maximally useful form, mankind's total image of itself and its environment." See Kochen's (1972) World Information Synthesis and Encyclopedia (WISE), or Worldwide Intelligence Service for the Development of Omniscience in Mankind (WISDOM). Kochen proposed in 1988 that the Library of Congress develop "the architecture for a pro-active electronic system based on content." It was a precise and comprehensive scheme whereby the Library of Congress might evolve into the national nucleus for the American part of the World Brain.

An integration of the world's knowledge. George Vladutz, formerly of the Soviet Union's VINITI system for coordinating current scientific knowledge, saw the World Brain in a "Global Exhaustive Scientific Concept Mapping and Linking System" of on-line, full-text, word-indexed documents. He said that "a particular aspect of the much larger social and cognitive endeavor we designate by the term World Brain is a system facilitating the integration of scientific knowledge, revealing in particular the differences and discrepancies in the understanding of the different scientific schools and thereby facilitating communication between related domains." Such a system, he says, is "within the reach of present-day data-processing technology as enriched by experience in citation analysis and word-concordance-based science mapping techniques" (reported by Andel 1987).

Here we might also mention the *noosphere* of Pierre Teilhard de Chardin (1964, 1969), in whose theory humanity's collective memory is passed on through education and "pulsating computers," research becoming the principal function of humanity, collective cerebralising into a brain; and the notion of *hyperintelligence* and collective memory (Bugliarello 1984), in which the human brain and computer power, millions of network nodes, come together for larger problem solving.

The accessibility of knowledge, such as the mechanically coordinated indexes for "universal bibliographical control" (Block 1984; Garfield 1968). Following up on the pioneering MEMEX system proposed by Vannevar Bush (1967), Eugene Garfield sees the World Brain as now existing in combinations of many commercially available components and such automated projects of the Institute of Scientific Information (ISI). These include the *Atlas of Science, Atlas of Biochemistry* and *Scientific Citation*

Index, which have thesaurus-type searching by word-map frequencies and bibliographic coupling and desktop computer access.

The World Brain is seen as an effort to bring together all four of the above dimensions. We note the "General Problem Solver" project at Carnegie Mellon in the 1970s, the Stanford University Heuristic Programming Project, and artificial intelligence projects such as MYCIN, a diagnosis program for physicians. These were predecessors of the project of a research consortium in Texas—Microelectronics and Computer Technology Corporation—which moves toward the kind of encyclopedic intelligence proposed by Wells. This consortium project is described as an effort to "encode and represent a summary of all the world's knowledge in an intelligent system." Glynn Harmon (1988) reported that the "team had completed the initial coding and entry of about 400 mutually distinct types of articles from the *Concise Columbia Encyclopedia*," which were to serve as "the basic frames" for encoding 30,000 more articles, a data base of "empirical facts, beliefs, heuristics, scripts, [and] mixed representations."

Harmon said that the Texas project aspired to the vision of the director of the project that "the power of intelligence may be based more on vast stores of broad and specialized knowledge about complex problem-solving environments [rather] than on elaborate reasoning processes." Also, he said, it is intended to be a monolith system that would store all the knowledge in one place.

The World Brain, however, is actually emerging as a complex, inter-related system, distributed in many networks and computers all over the world.

HISTORY OF THE IDEA

H.J.A. Goodman, a monitor and historian of the development of the World Brain concept, prefers to describe its history in terms of the evolution of some specific components in what is still a visionary movement (1987). A thorough history of the World Brain idea, he says, would trace its roots to the development of the first libraries in ancient Alexandria and Greece, where the idea of gathering, sorting, and storing of all information probably began.

Then perhaps it could be traced to the seventeenth century theologian and educator John Amos Comenius (1657) who had the idea for a Pan-sophic College that would bring together leading scholars to organize a comprehensive encyclopedia of all knowledge. Comenius—who almost became the first president of Harvard University—tied his concept to the idea of universal education and literacy so that all people might flower culturally and develop as informed citizens. Evidence is lacking as to whether Comenius had some influence on the development of the

5,000-volume *Great Chinese Encyclopedia,* which began in the eighteenth century. Goodman is certain, however, that Comenius influenced the French Encyclopedists and the establishment of the World Brain-like institutions that began to appear in Europe and America at the end of the nineteenth century. (For a summary of more history, see Bolter 1991.)

The first specific World Brain plans began about a hundred years ago when, with considerable financial backing and encouragement from the Belgian government, especially Senators Otlet and LaFontaine (Rayward 1975), the Universal Bibliographical Repertory was created to have a catalog card for every printed book. This led to the first comprehensive effort to create a universal system for the classification of knowledge, namely the Dewey Decimal system (now called the Universal Decimal System) for libraries. The repertory in Belgium became the predecessor of the International Federation for Documentation. Its unofficial American branch, the American Documentation Institute, in turn became the American Society for Information Science (ASIS).

That repertory in Belgium was also the predecessor and model for the League of Nations' Intellectual Cooperation Organization, which was the predecessor of UNESCO. Some members of the World Brain group think that UNESCO should become a directing and funding agency for more coordinated World Brain research and development, or even that UNESCO should itself become the World Brain.

Anticipating the collapse of League of Nations-sponsored activities as a result of events culminating in World War II, Wells wrote *World Brain* (1938) to advocate a new institution to cope with all available knowledge (hoping this might help prevent the war.) He thought that the process would eventually produce what he called a World Mind, that is, an outlook on life or a state of mind common to virtually all humans, one which would incorporate all the various elements of the World Brain concept.

A major advance towards the World Brain came with the arrival of electronic computer technology. Many new ideas and possibilities for the World Brain began to emerge, for example, the computer-based system proposed in 1963 by Douglas Engelbart, a conceptual framework for the augmentation of human intellect.

Watson Davis, the principal founder of ASIS, soon after the publication of *World Brain,* gave full support to Wells' idea, seeking to have ASIS become an instrument to help realize the concept (Davis 1967). He once expressed his frustration over why it was taking so long to materialize four important concepts that had promising beginnings right after World War II:

- one big global library;
- on-demand publication;

- one global scholarly journal;
- and the World Brain—a system to manage human knowledge.

These visions now begin to come together in the development of a worldwide electronic university.

Finally, in 1975, a World Mind research group was founded by Kochen, Goodman, and others. With a membership of prominent scholars in twelve countries, this group matured at a colloquium at Banff in Canada in 1979, with some people participating from a distance via audio or on-line computer conferencing. Although the group was inactive for a time in the early 1980s, members continued to conduct research and write papers and books related to the World Brain idea. Since 1987, the idea's development has been furthered through annual and midyear meetings at conferences of the ASIS, through a newsletter, and through the activities of the World Brain group within ASIS.

SOME ELECTRONIC COMPONENTS

Technology until recently was not ready to accomplish the vision of Wells. Now, however, satellites, optic fiber cables, neural networks, and parallel processing, able to unite thousands of computers from the smallest to the largest, make possible great advances in interdisciplinary cooperation and the coordination of knowledge. A simple way to show what is actually happening is to list some of the electronic components that are now important facilitators of World Brain developments.

Data Bases

The world's knowledge is rapidly going on-line in various computer data bases such as professional (law, medicine); university, public, and national library systems; and commercial. At one time it seemed like an impossible task to type into computer data bases all existing documents, but now the process is enhanced by optical scanning, which puts a book or article into a computer data base by photographing it page by page. Librarians increasingly cross-index such on-line information by word, subject, and clusters of related ideas. There are plans for coding all the world's knowledge by human needs and problems as well as by topics, authors, and words (See Hilton 1967). Rather than one global centralized encyclopedia as envisioned by Wells and others, the information core of the World Brain is dispersed into hundreds of thousands of interconnected information systems.

Interconnections and Software

Dispersed data bases are increasingly interconnected through global information utilities (computer networks) so that they are or could be available to all libraries and individuals. Software is now being developed to bring various systems together and to provide for simultaneous automatic computer translation, thereby heightening accessibility.

Hypertext and Hypermedia

These are computer systems that enable a scholar to manage interrelationships between ideas, diagrams, charts, and even sounds within distributed information. "Hyperties" (an interactive encyclopedia system; see Bolter 1991), for example, facilitates links between individual items of information to help a student navigate through complicated information systems. "The most difficult task is providing the conceptual overview" (Arms 1990).

Electronic Hypertext and Hypermedia Encyclopedias

Some experiments now begin to include sound, films, and graphics, so that the cross-indexed information is not merely printed. TV news and documentaries, as well as films, are made available on CD-ROM, videotape, and other digital means of storage. Reports on research that facilitate World Brain development, found in papers presented at ASIS and other professional meetings, include an article by Robert J. Glushko (1990) entitled "Designing a Hypertext Electronic Encyclopedia." In the system described in this article, any user can trace an idea through articles, pictures, diagrams, cross-references, bibliography papers, and videotapes and films. The system involves automatic translation, indexing, automatic coding, and continual updating and endless expansion. Each of a thousand such research papers may advance the idea only a tiny step, but such research, as it comes together, steadily moves towards a more fully realized World Brain.

Expert Systems and Artificial Intelligence

Computer programs that encode the expertise of specialists and that seek to "think" like human beings are World Brain components and enablers (Harmon 1988). Some people scoff when the proposed coordination of all the world's knowledge is thought of as solely electronic, as simply a coordination of knowledge by bringing together all of the world's computer data bases. A brain does not just store information, they say, it thinks. Even if expert systems and software facilitate so-called "thinking machines" (to relate, compare, and integrate all the world's information), this capability would still be only one facet of the World Brain.

STATUS OF THE WORLD BRAIN IDEA TODAY

In October 1988, on the fiftieth anniversary of the publication of the Wells book (at the ASIS annual meeting in Boston), a panel of members of the World Brain group reported on the extent to which what Wells proposed is, at the end of this century, coming into being.

H.J.A. Goodman described the unfolding of the World Brain idea in three basic types of research during the fifty years since Wells first proposed it:

- developments in theory and technology that further the idea, often serendipitously or unintentionally;
- intentional research;
- and research on strategy and tactics, "the exploration of possible implementation scenarios."

These contributions of researchers and others, Goodman says, together comprise a complex jigsaw puzzle, some pieces of which do not yet fit together, and some pieces of which are missing because they have not yet been created. Researchers and practitioners, however, now have in their hands many of the pieces of this "holographic puzzle-like model, which still lacks crystallization, coordination, integration, and articulation."

INTERCONNECTIONS AND INTEGRATION

The ASIS group seeks to bring together many mental pictures, images, and visions of the World Brain and interconnect them. For no matter how the World Brain is defined, *interconnections* must be a first key word in both electronic university and World Brain developments: interconnections of all the world's knowledge and information; among all scholars and research institutions; and between powerful kinds of technology such as computers of all sizes, global television, and other international communication systems.

When the human brain is used as an analogy, many such elements are seen as beginning to come together to make up synapses of the World Brain. Each day new connections are made. Someone may now perhaps write an article entitled "Globally interconnected networks are the connecting synapses of the World Brain."

The emerging World Brain, among other things, is a multi-way sharing of information so that, for example, the data base of local history of every community in the world is part of the global library of information, and can be used in "trade" to help pay for local use of global data bases. This can be illustrated by two very diverse projects: the Venice, Florida, public library collection of local genealogy, and the British multimedia DOMESDAY BOOK project, initiated by the BBC in London, in which school pupils all over England prepared multimedia information about their communities for electronic library use.

The World Brain, however, consists of *integration* of knowledge as well as interconnections. As part of his work, Goodman has been one of the catalysts who across more than two decades has been trying to bring together both the main ideas and the related technologies required to advance the implementation of the World Brain. This involves including nonprint media along with print media in the World Brain; proposing the need for a "measuring instrument . . . to determine the effectiveness and efficiency of the World Brain organism so that its viability could be maintained through continuous revision and upgrading" (See the *Encyclopedia of Library and Information Science* 1977); developing the REGISTER III system "of what the World Brain should look like and should be able to do"; along with Debons (Goodman and Debons 1991), proposing and developing a "Senior Scholars project" as a method for international collaborative scholarly work to get all knowledge on-line and integrated (see also Rossman 1982).

NEXT: ORGANIZING ALL THE WORLD'S KNOWLEDGE

Technocrats and scholars are now at work on bits and pieces of what may become the most important research project in history, one that may involve nearly every university and every scholar: the computerizing, indexing, and organizing of all knowledge. This massive scholarly project, underway but not yet systemized or coordinated, can provide one of the most important foundations for a new and more adequate system of global scholarship, research, and higher education.

This process is taking place in data bases dispersed in computers all over the world. As such data bases become interconnected and cross-indexed, the next step may be the emergence of a comprehensive organization of human knowledge that will continually learn and adapt, with a greater potential than was ever imagined by the ancient Greeks, Comenius, or even Wells or Bush. It may in time begin to take down the national and other boundaries between universities and scholarly disciplines, and also between the scientist-scholar and the average educated person, while at the same time cherishing the unique contributions of each culture and nation. We may thus stand on the threshold of an era in higher education when any educated student can be empowered to assume a more significant share in the testing and advancement of knowledge.

How is this great research project to be accomplished? Who will do the work and how? Some of it is underway in many universities, but a comprehensive scheme is needed.

A first proposal was an article on "The Coming Great Electronic Encyclopedia" (Rossman 1982), which proposed that scholars in the professional associations of each discipline (and in each subdivision of each research area) begin by preparing a definitive research article. Once online it could be regularly updated and could be endlessly expanded. One such model was the Human Area Relations Files project (at Yale) in anthropology, which was set up regularly to integrate all new research data. Rather than adding each new book or paper as a library does, it made only corrections or added what was not already in the data base.

A more significant model, perhaps, is the Online Mendelian Inheritance in Man (OMIM) project at Welch Medical Library, Johns Hopkins University. Two sites are responsible for keeping OMIM comprehensive and up-to-date: the Imperial Cancer Research Center in London and the German Cancer Research Center in Heidelberg. The system makes it possible for any scientist who uses the data to "make a point in the text" (Lucier 1990). These posted annotations are then reviewed by the OMIM staff to see which should be permanently added.

Much of the work of continually updating the data base in each field could be assigned to advanced Ph.D. students whose term papers and dissertations could examine the data base, proposing weak points to be corrected, new information to be added, and suggestions for next steps in research. Doctoral candidates could thus debate such points with each other, perhaps electronically, wherever in the world other students might be working on similar topics. Their scholarly preparation could be greatly aided by continuing to converse on-line to clarify disagreements, issues, alternatives, and theses.

Enlarging that proposal, Goodman and Anthony Debons (1991) have designed a Senior Scholars Project which has been endorsed by many university administrators and prominent scholars in various countries. It would empower and authorize retired scholars for the initial task of eliminating the duplication of current knowledge in each research area, first preparing and then continuously updating a definitive statement of the "state of the art" of knowledge in their respective fields.

Retiring scholars would be invited to make use of some of their most productive retirement years. Instead of feeling "put out to pasture" such scholars could—in return for their participation—be provided with computer and communications facilities, laboratory access, interlibrary loan facilities, and in time perhaps a sophisticated electronic workstation that would automatically do such routine work as comprehensive indexing.

This Senior Scholar's "State of the Art" Project would also build an evaluation mechanism into the system itself. The process of organizing, coding, synthesizing, and updating knowledge in a particular area would also involve an adequate peer assessment process.

INDIVIDUALIZATION

This organization of all the world's knowledge could be aided by a more individualized/custom-tailored kind of research assistance, which is one of the most important aspects of World Brain development, and is one of Goodman's main contributions to the concept and its implementation. Such tailoring, based on individual and group user information needs, has been facilitated by findings in cognitive psychology, by library and other research on user information needs, by developments in artificial intelligence and expert systems, by advances in automatic indexing and translation, and by hypermedia encyclopedias. He says, "the increasing abilities of computers... have rendered ever more closely possible the composition of individual and group profiles or models of individual minds, virtual alter egos."

A major attempt in this direction is being made at the MIT Media Lab (Brand 1987), where work continues on a system to automatically sort through visual and audio material, such as all new journal articles and research papers. On the basis of a selective dissemination system, and by means of a regularly updated information profile of all of a scholar's research interests and projects, it will call to the individual's attention any references found in the vast sources of data available that are appropriate to that scholar's work.

Young scholars of today can, at the beginning of their careers, begin to use computers to cross-index all of their lecture notes, reviews, and research papers. Then one of these days an "expert system" will automatically be able to tag for their personal "body of knowledge and research" every relevant item in the encyclopedic World Brain related to a particular research area. As all scholars begin to relate to the World Brain in this organized way, a solid foundation will begin to emerge for "grand research designs", for highly significant research uses of the World Brain, even before it is fully in existence.

The "greatest scholarly project in history" so far is that of getting all knowledge coordinated on-line, whether by the Goodman/Debons proposed method or some other. It can increasingly be facilitated by interdisciplinary committees that have strong representation from major universities and professional associations in all countries.

WHERE NEXT: SOME PROBLEMS AND BARRIERS

Much of this review of World Brain history and developments is summarized from reports of the 1990 and 1987 ASIS panels (Andel 1987), the latter on the fiftieth anniversary of the H. G. Wells idea. At that 1987 session, Goodman reported a great need to prevent undesirable happenings, occurrences that might propel the World Brain in wrong directions, or which might result in undesirable forms.

Manfred Kochen, in response, said that "for good or evil the World Brain is now being born, whether humanity wants it yet or not." Therefore, he said, adequate World Brain developments now require

- vision, that is, an intention about what to do;
- mobilization of capacity, that is, who is to do what;
- commitment, political will, and willingness of scholars to undertake a great task;
- and then, of course, management, coordination, and integration to do it right.

The same might be said as well of many other aspects of the emerging electronic university.

If all of Kochen's stipulations come to pass, they would make it possible to deal with a number of important World Brain questions that are now being raised:

1. Rights and privileges need to be legally safeguarded. Needed rights include: property rights protection for the creators of new information; protection from "information colonialism" for people in the developing nations and less privileged people everywhere (the information poor); and information freedom for all (access to information) without having to worry about invasion of privacy.

Ted Nelson's Xanadu (1987) and the Goodman-Debons Senior Scholars plan both stipulate procedures whereby the creators of information can register their names and the nature of their novel information and so be protected from later claims by others to be the originators. The involvement of private universities and business-sponsored data bases can hopefully help guarantee freedom for the global encyclopedia from government censorship.

2. An agency is needed to coordinate World Brain plans and to develop a system to coordinate all knowledge. Perhaps this will be the structure that emerges as a research section of the emerging worldwide electronic university. Meanwhile, the World Brain and the electronic university are both developing without a comprehensive plan. Scholars have yet to transcend or deregulate the barriers caused by the jealousy, blindness, and ignorance of competing governments, competing universities, business corporations, and the ambitions of individual researchers and scientists.

3. This points to political and philosophical issues: who will control? That is, who will administer the system and how can it be prevented

from becoming a monopoly of some sort, public or private, and not available to all. And what principles will determine what is included or left out? Harmon reminded the 1987 ASIS panelists that there is another crucial problem in the development of "encyclopedic intelligence"; that is, what world views should govern the organization of encyclopedic knowledge bases? Ralph Dumain, who has been examining uses of computers in philosophy, asked if the World Brain idea is more appropriate for the natural sciences than for the humanities or the social sciences and expressed concern about subjective issues of power, social control, and politics.

4. Lack of funding limits a more organized development of the World Brain, as does the unwillingness of competing governments, agencies, and universities to work together. Funding agencies have not supported projects such as the proposal by Kochen for the Library of Congress or the now closed Alexandria Institute (named for the great ancient library). Perhaps the Institute should not have attempted so large a task with limited funds, but its brochures stated an inspiring vision: "to significantly change the way to explore knowledge [by] capturing all the world's recorded knowledge and making it available as needed." Perhaps funding for "the great scholarly project" will come from business corporations since the World Brain will be important for business, especially for the international trade in information.

5. Is getting all human knowledge on-line, coordinating, organizing, and synthesizing it, too large a task to ever be accomplished? Especially since each year's new research now becomes an overburdening percentage of the preexisting whole? And how will overload be managed, especially if many interdisciplinary areas continue to be developed (Pagels 1988)?

It can be managed, it can be done, when a system is in place so that the world's scholars can cooperate. Millions of collaborators can do together what none can do alone. The scope of the task will also be more manageable when duplication of publication is reduced. A large number of research monographs, now produced for professional advancement in the university system, are rarely cited or used by other scholars. If this is because other scholars do not know about a paper, a World Brain system can correct that. If it is because the scholarship is not adequate, if it adds nothing new to knowledge, then a World Brain system can clarify this in two ways: only what is verifiable will be incorporated, and there can be much less pedantic research when a scholar can use the global electronic encyclopedia to see who else—anywhere in the world— is doing what and what next needs to be done; that is, what research projects, large or small, might make a significant contribution.

6. We seem to be entering a time when human beings can create technology to do whatever is needed. The problem is with us human

beings in the poverty of our vision and imagination. Some motivation for World Brain coordination will probably come from overload on professional associations and from humanity's inability to deal otherwise with crucial issues. How else can humanity keep up with the enlarging scope of global problems? Karl Schneider of the U.S. National Agriculture Library and selected in 1990 to be the editor of the ASIS World Brain group's on-line newsletter, has suggested to the ASIS panel that the current global ecological crisis might provide the powerful motivation for enlarging and developing the World Brain. Panelist George Vladutz added that one of the primary functions of the human brain is to ensure the survival of an individual; so also, he said, the World Brain is needed to insure the survival of humanity. It is hard to imagine, he said, that the World Brain could actually solve many of the problems we read about in *Pravda* or the *Washington Post* but "it will reveal them, focus on them, and help analyze them."

7. Will the World Brain be a problem-solving system? A human brain, of course, does more than store information, more than index and compare it. It creates new ideas, systems, and syntheses, has creative imagination, creates mental models of reality, and creates and solves problems. As more information is exchanged among neurons, as during a dream, the more likely it is that creative ideas will emerge. So too the World Brain will hopefully help humanity solve larger and larger problems, such as how to provide adequate food, health care, and education for every person in the world. The universities will need to provide the more powerful and sophisticated thinking and research that the World Brain can help to enable. Again the word is *interconnections*. The World Brain, with the assistance of integrated information and telecommunication technologies, can bring together the skills and expertise of hundreds and thousands of people, fusing a network of minds into a World Brain.

8. Is the World Brain merely a tool for the universities to use? Of course it is a tool, but no more so than universities or encyclopedias or any other human institution. And is the university, and especially the emerging international electronic university, part of the World Brain? As for now, it seems that even if universities let control of the great research project for organizing and coordinating all knowledge slip into the hands of business corporations for profit, the university and its scholars will not only use the World Brain, they will be essential components of it. Universities are thus part of the World Brain and its emergence may totally reshape them.

To repeat, despite all that can be said about the technology that is making the World Brain possible, *the crucial element is human.* Pursuing the analogy to the human brain, the interconnected scholars, mostly at universities, now constitute the electricity that causes a "brainstorm," the "chemical" elements in the collective intelligence. Thus the "electricity" that sparks the connections, that makes creativity and thought possible, comes from people and universities—those who do all the library research and organization-of-information work that is bringing the World Brain into existence.

9. Will the World Brain have a heart? Richard Kirby and others at a conference in Britain on the World Brain see a religious aspect to the concept, suggesting with Teilhard de Chardin that the World Brain must, as envisioned by Comenius, empower and serve the needs of all the people in the world. Kirby and Stephen Rosen of the City University of New York (Kirby and Rossman 1990) call for a "world heart," proposing that some of the impulses that activate the emerging World Brain are love (at least the love of truth and humanity) and the quest for wholeness (the fact that all sciences, all data are interconnected).

10. Can the World Brain organize possible and future ideas also? And in such a way as to invite all people in the world to share? Stan Pokras of the Public Interest Media Project and Gregory Wright of the *Brain/ Mind Bulletin* (Wright and Pokras 1990) have called for humanity "to put on its collective thinking cap" and initiate a process of society-wide brainstorming. To provide a place where anyone's creative ideas might be preserved and expanded, they propose *IdeaNet* "for big ideas and little ideas, grand proposals and light-hearted divertissements, sweeping schemes and incremental improvements to existing things and ways— and the people who create them." Ideas would be cross-indexed with a manager in each category to help organize and interrelate creative ideas.

Since so many good ideas are lost, they propose "a global suggestion box," a place where ideas can be posted "where they will be seen by the largest possible number of intelligent and possibly interested individuals, organizations, companies and projects." This, they say, is "idea husbandry," raising something from seed so it can grow and develop.

It seems at times, unfortunately, that the World Brain (and also the international electronic university) are emerging in ways analogous to Marvin Minsky's (Kolata 1991) view of the human brain as a "kludge," that is, something that is clumsy or patched together, an illogical network of connections. Nevertheless, despite humanity's often illogical and contradictory behavior, human brains, singly and in concert, have produced ideas for a logically organized World Brain, world encyclopedia, world mind, and world electronic university. Now on the horizon perhaps there also are responsible and empowering entities that embody all these ideas and ideals.

The next chapter discusses the electronic classroom and how an online teacher functions in the midst of this complexity.

Eight

THE GLOBAL CLASSROOM AND INSTRUCTOR

The goal of the multimedia Electronic Campus is to have full-motion video, high resolution still images and graphics, audio-program material and text all coexist in digital form . . . through communication networks . . . The system consists of four major components: the user's workstation, the fiber-optic distribution network, playback equipment and a fourth-generation Technology Access Governor . . . capable of controlling many technologies from remote locations via fiber-optic cable.

G. C. Elmore 1991

Perhaps "classroom" is not the word to use, at least for the place in which a professor meets with a student on another continent via TV or computer conference. Linda Harasim (1990) prefers to say that "online education is a *new environment*, with new attributes and requires new approaches to understand, design and implement it." She also points out that this new environment, in which geographically separated learners meet, can be one that encourages social interaction and group process. In other words, a "new kind of classroom" can be created as computer-mediated communication (CMC) begins to offer "study and work environments for groups of users rather than simple tools for individual work."

It was only natural, she says, for early efforts to be modeled either on the correspondence course or on the typical campus lecture hall. Now, however, why not electronic classrooms modeled on the college music studio, theatre, chemistry or physics laboratory, agricultural greenhouse, or foreign language studio?

The instructor who retired only a few years ago may now be astonished to visit a classroom that has rows of computers so that each student recites as often as he or she wishes, and where the instructor can continually monitor the responses of each student. It can be even more surprising to realize that some class members may be in another city or country. The teacher can project onto the students' computer screens some image or data from a distant museum or library, then a film from a space satellite, or a lecture from an expert in another country. A student halfway around the world can also watch and participate.

THE TELEVISION CLASSROOM

An international meeting of university presidents, reported in chapter 1, pointed to the emergence of a "truly global classroom" based on relatively low-cost technologies. Did they have in mind the sort of convocation or assembly that draws together large numbers of students on campus to hear a visiting celebrity? At present there are many types of electronic classrooms and different combinations will be used as appropriate to different courses, cultures, and situations: TV classrooms, on-line computer network classrooms, and combinations of the two (Mason and Kaye 1990). Also there are more effective possibilities down the road.

The television classroom uses regular TV for lectures and discussion, as was done in the joint history course between Tufts and Moscow universities. On cable TV a lecture can be offered to thousands, even millions of students. The lecturer can use motion pictures and slides to enliven and clarify the presentation, can interview experts, or show laboratory demonstrations in other countries. This kind of lecture by expert teachers can be recorded on videotape in cooperation with the researchers/scientists who know the most about the subject, wherever in the world they may be. Such lectures via TV or cable, on videotape or videodisc, or even on audiotape or over the telephone, can be used to bring reports of the latest research into even the best universities and, especially when better options are not available, new educational resources to individual learners in their homes or at their places of work.

When such a lecture is live on TV, as in Michael Catchpole's (1986) one-way video and two-way audio system—known as interactive television—students at home can participate via telephone, as on some commercial TV shows. This gives distance students the opportunity (at the price of a long-distance call) to ask a question or make a comment.

A teaching assistant can screen the calls, interrupting when the question is pertinent, or rearranging the order of questions as best for the course procedure. Catchpole uses TV language as he tells of his experience conducting a TV course: "producing" a course and "hosting" it. He points out that a teacher needs different instructional and production skills in order to prepare a TV course.

Good teaching, he found, involved more than a TV lecture. The instructor, or the team preparing the course, needed TV production skills as well as skills in using and appearing before TV cameras. A student manual (textbook, pacing schedule for completing assignments and exams) was sent by mail. The student was also sent videotapes for study use, supplementing the TV presentations. These were presentations, not just lectures, in that experts were interviewed, graphics and films were used, and learners went on TV field trips. Since most people have the habit of relaxing for entertainment in front of a TV set, students were encouraged to watch from a table, to take notes, and in other ways to turn their rooms into classrooms.

Ralph Coppola (1991) reports on pilot projects, using varied combinations of technology in which instructors interact with prominent scientists. Students then use interactive videodisc for exploring the solar system, design a robot space probe to go to a planet such as Mars, and lastly simulate data collection by using "actual data accumulated by scientists in fly-bys of the planet." They then can use "remotely sensed information from Earth to compare the planet they've analyzed to the Earth." Nursing students similarly use interactive video to simulate crisis situations, then two-way audio conferencing for discussion and asking questions, and finally a real-time TV link for active participation in a real emergency-room situation. With two-way monitors they can see whatever doctors and nurses are doing. It was determined that these students learned "twice the information in half the time as compared to traditional information presentation techniques."

THE "VIRTUAL CLASSROOM"

Another kind of classroom, now more available to the distance student, brings students and instructor together on a computer network. The lecturer in the usual campus class may find students frustrated by the limited time available for asking questions. Sitting at their computer terminals, all students can "speak" as often as they wish. They can insert any question at the time they think of it. It may not be answered right then, but it need not be neglected as is often the case in a classroom where time limits the number of questions. Participation can thus be much more active, less passive, and the learners can be much more in control of the environment and the learning process so as to meet their own needs and interests (Turoff and Hiltz 1988; Rasmussen, Bang, and Lunby 1991).

An interactive class (group process and discussion) can be created in this "worldwide virtual classroom" if the instructor learns how. The technology, the emerging new tools to empower the class, can convert the network into a social environment. Students talk with each other as much as they wish. Courses can provide "an environment that engages students in authentic educational activities" (Newman 1990). The term "virtual classroom" is copyrighted and therefore should be used only to refer to the use of the licensed software system for teaching and learning first developed on the EIES (Electronic Information Exchange System) based at the New Jersey Institute of Technology. Its developers, Murray Turoff and S. R. Hiltz (1988) called this "new means of educational delivery for college-level and postgraduate professional education [a] teaching and learning space located with a computer-mediated communications system." The Annenberg/CBP Project provided funds for its creation, implementation, evaluation, refining, and demonstration to make it possible to do globally what happens in a traditional class, plus "to produce interactive, didactic group learning activities, which improve on the typical class by making it more convenient, by providing more active participation, and self-pacing on the part of the learner." It provided "class conferences" where students and teacher could meet on-line, a message system for private communications among them, and special software for activities such as tests and the creation and display of graphics. There could thus be constant interaction with feedback from the teacher wherever appropriate (see Hiltz 1988a, 1988b).

Paul Levinson (1988, 1990), who has had a great deal of experience with students from other countries taking courses from New York via his ConnectEd program, points to "the web of social expectations and consequences." It is a great mistake, he says, to compare his on-line classes to correspondence courses, which provide nothing like the interaction with other students possible on a computer network. However, the environment is created not by the technology, but by "social engineers" who learn to use it well. The students can be almost anywhere on earth, he says, and one big advantage of courses on a computer network is enhanced personal attention and participation. The instructor can stimulate a kind of personal engagement and self-directed learning that are becoming rare today on campuses.

Levinson therefore strongly resists the idea of electronic education being a mass assembly-line process. When asked how he would set up a course for a thousand students, he refused to consider ten tutors with a hundred students each. An on-line class, he insisted, should not have more than twenty-five students. which he finds to be the maximum number for any class if good teaching and learning are to take place.

A quite different set of skills are needed by the on-line teacher. In contrast to a TV course, or distance education via radio in the Third World, the virtual classroom also assumes a kind of teamwork among teachers, students, those who prepare the course materials, and the technicians. Where the TV course seems similar to the ordinary college classroom in that it tends to be lecture-based, the on-line ConnectEd course is mostly text-based and thus the student is less tempted to drift into TV's entertainment mode. Special software can make it easy for the student to connect with the computer network system for study and instruction at any time of the day or night, and in principle, at almost any place in the world.

We will illustrate with two cases. The first is a spring 1990 Freshman Composition class (Jaeger 1990). Research on quality, methods, and problems that arose in the course found that "even with such an overwhelmingly autonomous group . . . instructor and student must stay in contact." By regularly monitoring student participation, the instructor found that he sometimes needed to send E-mail reminders, or make occasional personal phone calls to offer encouragement and help. However, "working individually or personally with students does not have to mean 'in person.' " Quality performance, he found, did not require the kind of socializing that goes on in most classrooms. The quality of instruction was superior to similar groups in class; he said, "teaching on-line can and does foster a sense of closeness between student and instructor."

While some students dropped out—about the same percentage as in a typical college class—because they changed jobs, became ill or whatever, the main problem the instructor faced was frustration over a "balky (computer delivery) system." This meant that a successful on-line classroom requires regular technological assistance and support for the instructor. When more trouble-free technology was provided, student satisfaction was as high as among students on campus.

George Jaeger found that "teaching an online class takes minimally two to three times longer than teaching in a classroom." In a study of faculty and administrators participating in an Annenberg/CPB Project evaluation, however, it was found that electronic courses were neither harder nor easier for teachers; that students performance was equal, with electronic courses showing higher retention rates; that electronic courses helped students to experience real-world problems in a safer and more cost-effective manner; and that the classes were easily manageable for the instructor.

A second illustration is provided by Paul Levinson (1988) in a transcript of an on-line course entitled "Popular Culture and the Media." When his students in other countries enrolled, they received clear instructions on how to participate in the following campus resources on the computer network:

- the "cafe" for recreational conversation;

- the technical forum to get help if any problems were experienced with telephone lines, computers, software, etc.;
- the library to read assigned papers;
- the bookstore to order texts and audio and video tapes through the on-line book service;
- tutoring (for students whose second language is English);
- counseling about future employment;
- and, of course, class for lectures and discussion.

With simple keystrokes the new student could easily find and use class assignments, topics, definitions, and text material.

Students were first encouraged to introduce themselves to the instructor and other members of the class by typing in biographical information. The instructor responded to their expressed needs, interests, and questions and encouraged students to do so with each other. The transcript of interaction shows that some students responded to an invitation to "meet me for a drink and some personal conversation at the on-line cafe" and some did not.

THE TELECLASS OR TELECONFERENCING CLASS

Another kind of electronic class combines the best features of the computer network "virtual classroom" with interactive TV, using both a computer network and television (although generally the less expensive slow-scan TV that can be sent over ordinary telephone lines). The GU registered term for this procedure is "global lecture hall (GLH)." One demonstration of this kind of electronic classroom took place in July 1986, at the World Future Society's conference on managing complexity. Takeshi Utsumi's GLOSAS/GU project showed how to use slow-scan TV so that students and instructors in various countries could see each other during a lecture or discussion; facsimile for the exchange of text, spread sheets, and charts; and the EIES computer network to organize and manage the "classroom." Because the students were in both Japan and North America, the computer conferencing system was also used to help people in two languages communicate effectively with each other. (Computer translation is now being developed so that what is said in Japanese over the telephone can be heard in English or other languages.) All of the lecture material and discussion was summarized on-line, which also meant it could later be reviewed and studied at leisure. This information was also projected onto large electronic screens where groups were gathered together in the same room.

This demonstration involved students in several countries, showing how learners could share in a dialog among the leading experts in a field. At a second such GLH demonstration, in November 1987, students in nine countries and teachers in three acted as if they were all in the same room. This "model course" was managed from a studio/lecture hall at the Massachusetts Institute of Technology (MIT), participants watching each other on a slow-scan TV camera. The author of this book, coordinating the demonstration from a computer terminal at MIT, invited the participants to imagine themselves in "the classroom of the future." The demonstration used the facilities of NHK television in Japan and the EIES computer network to connect instructors in Hawaii, San Diego, and Fort Collins, Colorado (Colorado State University) and to involve students from around the rim of the Pacific—including Korea, Guam, Australia, Japan—and other cities spanning fourteen time zones and two calendar dates. While the demonstration was set up to find what the problems might be, and some serious ones were found, most of the participants were able to interact in this "global lecture hall" as if they were in the same location.

One lecturer, invited by NASA to lecture to people at several locations, using slow-scan TV, said that he missed the two-way eye contact which is the only way he can be sure that students from other cultures and languages understand what he is saying. However, that lecturer had not used a computer network to supplement slow-scan TV so that participants could anonymously ask questions and make comments during the presentation. He concluded that for some kinds of lectures, where laboratory work is presented, for example, slow-scan TV may need to be replaced with a video conferencing system where all students can continually see and be seen.

In other words, it is important for the technicians to be actively involved in planning the combination of technologies adequate to do the job in each unique situation. Much of this process can be automated in a specially designed building or electronic classroom, a studio or "situation room," which is specially equipped for the purpose.

THE SITUATION ROOM

Some instruction now begins to take place in electronic studio-classrooms and/or laboratories, "empowering environments" (Glenn 1989) especially designed for distance education. The term "situation room" generally applies to a military command center that brings together in one place all of the information, electronic maps, data bases, and computer and communications technology needed for directing a military operation. Some multinational corporations also have such situation rooms that bring together all the technology, software, and information needed for business management and instruction. Such a studio, especially designed for electronic course instruction (preparation, transmission, and receiving), first simply includes all that is needed for studying and teaching a particular subject: books, computers to connect to electronic encyclopedias and data bases, videotape and CD-ROM players, telephone connections, and electronic blackboards. More sophisticated situation rooms can make use of computer simulations, "scientific visualization, graphical user interfaces, hypertext, hypermedia, object-oriented programming and visual languages," (Spring 1990) and many other kinds of technology especially designed to empower particular kinds of research or teaching.

The term situation room suggests a different combination of technologies for each different situation. For example, a medical student who is a continent away can watch a master surgeon operate, using camera eyes that may give a closer view than is possible for the student who stands beside the surgeon in the operating room. Students in one country can participate in a chemistry lab experiment taking place in another, watching, trying some of the experimentation themselves, and carrying on a conversation with the students and instructor in the distant laboratory. An electronic classroom designed for art or music (with, for example, something like the "creation station" developed at the University of Michigan) will therefore differ radically from one designed to teach agriculture. The music station can be used by composers in two countries to work together as if in the same room; and a student can play along with an orchestra that is rehearsing in another country. (See the December 3, 1990, *San Francisco Chronicle* on a joint orchestra concert involving musicians playing in three countries.)

COMPUTER-SIMULATED "VIRTUAL REALITY" CLASSROOM

It is important now to begin to prepare for many new and unexpected possibilities in higher education. For a moment let's move beyond what is now possible and happening to suggest how a student can "be even more present" in a class that is a thousand miles away. The technology already exists, and demonstrations show the possibilities of various kinds of computer-managed "intelligent classrooms." A *virtual reality* (simulated) classroom can enable a kind of education that more effectively uses all three ways in which people learn: the intellectual, the emotional (including art and imaging), and the kinesthetic (physical movement). Without leaving the actual classroom or home, students can travel through on-line simulations to distant museums, laboratories, or other cultures. David Traub (1990) proposes "virtual reality environments as an ideal milieu for learning," but laments the fact that they are likely to be first used in business, the military, and entertainment rather than in education "where . . . most needed." His "goal is a simulation-based environment that . . . maximizes the user's ability to control discovery." Myron Krueger (1983), building on his experience at creating virtual reality rooms and experiences for museums, describes how: physically handicapped students, confined at home, could through such a system "attend" a class, experiencing it as if really present; an entire class might "visit" and tour a museum in another city without leaving their classroom; virtual-reality technology could create a "history room" in which a scholar could enter a specific period of history or participate in a past event; two scholars separated by a great distance could share the same experience as if in the same room. Those interested in this technology and experimentation can find more detail in Krueger (1990) and his book *Artificial Reality*. (See also Laurel 1990; Walser 1990; Fisher 1990; Rheingold 1986; and Brand 1987.)

Howard Rheingold reminds us that as yet we only have glimpses and primitive experiments, such as Alan Kay's "fantasy amplifier" or the imaginative "vivarium," a virtual reality interdisciplinary learning place developed at MIT. What we see at present, he says, is like people at the turn of the century trying to understand the future possibilities of film by watching some of the first silent movies. With some amusement, he reminds us that when asked what TV might be used for, one of its inventors proposed that it would be used largely in hospitals to monitor patients.

After the virtual reality classroom, the next step may be a specially designed "virtual global electronic campus." The Japanese and Australian governments are currently researching the idea of a "world university" which would center in a "multimedia network . . . building on Japanese and Australian strengths in information and communications technology." (WFS 1991) The network of computer, video, facsimile, and telephone systems would "create new options for learning" and would also "serve as an engine of technological innovation and economic growth." This electronic university would link universities and research institutions around the globe, and would include "a World Environmental Management Center with research stations ranging from aquaculture to waste management." Perhaps such a development in Australia can be a prototype/laboratory to experiment with what can then later be re-created, at much less cost, in Africa, South Asia, and Latin America. A consortium may do what the institutions of no one small country can do alone.

Until then, most of the world's instructors (whether teaching in or using resources from the worldwide electronic university) must be content with more modest technology. Research is underway and software is emerging, however, to make possible entirely new kinds of teaching and classroom management.

A successful worldwide electronic university will require a specialized workstation/teachstation (especially software) to build upon the automated office developed for business, which combines telephone, type-writer, files, and all other office instruments into one electronic system. The range of teaching software now being developed is remarkable, and can automate all the instructor's work in administration, evaluation, planning, testing, grading, tutoring, team coordinating (groupware), research, and technology management. This system can thus automate and make easy many of the instructional and management tasks required for effective distance teaching. Its authoring software, used to create special textbooks and teaching materials, could easily be adjusted for use in preparation for the virtual classroom; it could also bring together all materials needed for a particular class and organize them by date and topic. (For the handicapped, see Coombs 1989.)

A teachstation can make it possible for the instructor to supervise the participation of distant on-line students as easily as those in the conventional classroom. The instructor can be in close touch with students who are thousands of miles away and can automatically monitor whether or not they are comprehending the material, following the argument, or keeping up with assignments (Abrioux 1991).

The teachstation software now under development can have a "computer profile" (Brand 1987) of the instructor's teaching needs and his or her research projects and interests. One keystroke could call up all needed information, films, or graphics for any particular subject and instructional module. Demonstration experiments (Arms 1990) of "customized search profiles . . . specified by the user," make possible automatic searches of new data bases for any information the instructor ought to have. The system can "flag down" each item that is pertinent to the history, cultural context, and development of a particular research project.

The teachstation can help instructors organize knowledge so as to be more effective. Buckminster Fuller once instructed an office assistant at Southern Illinois State University to arrange an exhaustively cross-referenced, alphabetically coded, first-word index to all his topical concept files; then to package all the concepts to save him from repetitive discourse and writing. As a result (*Futurist*, Sept./Oct. 1987), all his lectures, including those on tape, his letters, unpublished papers, notebooks, drawings, blueprints, and clippings were brought together until they achieved a sort of self-organizing character that approached a new art form.

The instructor's teachstation could also regularly update a profile of each student, not just grades and record of work, but detailed information on needs, vocational plans, problems, and deficiencies. The teachstation could then help the instructor to personalize instructional plans and materials to meet the unique needs of individual students whether on campus or in other countries. Also, electronic textbooks can be designed for "continuous and periodic assessment" (Thorkildsen and Friedman 1984) so as to "present text questions, monitor and record test data, present immediate or intermittent feedback, present additional instruction, repeat instructions, provide correctional procedures for remediation," and "automatically track students' progress." For example, *Concepts in General Chemistry* (Weyh and Crook 1988) included a diagnostic error evaluation that pinpointed a student's mistakes at each instructional step. This was found to result in remarkable improvement in student mastery, for example, "in handling the most sophisticated types of equation writing." Caroline Arms (1990) reports the methods of Johns Hopkins University and many other universities to facilitate such processes. Such teachstation tools can free the instructors from many routine chores so that they can have more personal time to give to distant and nearby students.

TOWARD A NEW LEARNING/TEACHING STYLE

Robin Mason and Anthony Kaye (1990) describe the "mixed-model" in which a distant instructor may relate to students in a variety of modes. The community outside the college may become more involved in teaching as resource people scattered over a wide area are recruited for a network of tutors and advisors. The increasing success of electronic distance education has "already begun to change the nature and structure of present institutions in subtle ways" and this influence on higher education is likely to enlarge, changing traditional style of teaching, breaking down the walls between place-based and distance education, and creating "a network of scholars, space for collective thinking, and access to peers for socializing and serendipitous exchange" (Mason and Kaye 1990).

Greg Kearsley (1985) points out how instruction skills and the learning process change significantly from passive learning to active (see Yarrish 1991); from scheduled classes to individualized programs; from teacher-controlled to learner-controlled; from printed text to electronic materials; from memorizing to problem solving and decision making; from content-oriented to performance-oriented; and to provide specialized learning experiences for each unique individual instead of generalized instruction aimed at the average student.

Luke T. Young et al. (1988) describe how the university instructor a decade from now may use the computer network to keep in close touch with students and to prepare his teaching program each day. When he prepares a lecture, he first uses it with students who meet him on campus because he likes to meet and talk with students in person when he can, but he has many more students linked in from other locations on the computer network. Using an electronic blackboard that can be read in the classroom and also on computer screens in distant locations, he calls up maps, charts, graphs, or slides (even moving pictures) to illustrate his lecture. He can show a film stored in Berlin to students in South America and in Australia.

The lecture/presentation is recorded on videotape for later use by students who cannot attend while it is delivered and for those who want to review it again for study after class or in preparation for an exam later in the term. The professor may not present the lecture to a live class again, although he may assign it to other classes and continue to revise and update it. When it is ready then it may be "published," that is, made available for rent or sale for use anywhere with subtitles or translations into other languages. Before being thus published on interactive videodisc, it would be submitted to a peer review committee to see if it should be recommended for a global use. For "the tele-university will enable the best teachers to lecture to thousands of students at dozens of universities simultaneously" (Young et al. 1988). However, the real advantage is that eminent researchers will be able to teach extremely specialized courses to small groups scattered around the globe. "This has exciting possibilities for breaking down the barriers between institutions—geographically and politically" (Young et al. 1988). (Recommended reading: Sproull and Kiesler 1991; Kay 1991; and Cerf 1991 on groupware; Computer-supported Cooperative Work and Owen in Laurel 1990 on "technologists should be listening to artists.")

The next chapter will discuss textbooks for the worldwide electronic university.

Nine

ELECTRONIC TEXTBOOKS FOR THE DISTANCE STUDENT

... something of a cross between a sheet of paper and current laptop and palmtop computers ... Krivacic of PARC has built a prototype ... that uses ... a radio network with enough communications bandwidth to support hundreds of devices per person per room.

Mark Weiser 1991

Nintendo is ... potentially the ... major force for educational change. (Papert [of MIT] is working with Nintendo to understand better what children learn ...) On a network, these machines could change the face of our culture.

Nicholas Negroponte 1991

Much that a student needs to know is in the world's libraries, and chapter 6 reported how that information is increasingly available to students online. Yet it is impossible even for full-time researchers, in a field like chemistry, for example, to keep up with all the new discoveries and information in such a field each year. So apprentice learners turn to the university for the help of experts in each field in sorting out what they need to know, organizing the information and educational experiences in a helpful sequence, and so forth, in relation to individual students' personal and professional goals.

Traditionally, the university does this by packaging information and a process of learning into courses and textbooks. That process is now being transformed by electronic "textbooks" and "courseware" including all the lectures, readings, discussions, experiments, demonstrations, and even field trips. Textbook packages are more important than communications technology for the worldwide electronic university.

It is the job of Hiroshi Ishi (1990), "computer-supported cooperative work" researcher at the Human Interface Laboratories in Japan, "to help people think together, across boundaries of time, space and culture." His experience in academic groups such as the Association for Computing Machinery led him to be aware of "the importance of culture in the design of computer-supported communication tools." How people use tools is affected by culture, and software for international electronic education must be based on an adequate understanding of the nature of crosscultural communication. Now that "the telecommunications infrastructure for delivering powerful information tools to large numbers of people is being built," he says, "it is time to devote more effort to the human side of the system." People should interact *through* computers, not with them. Emerging high-speed networks and other communications technologies "have created the foundation for doing things with groups of people that haven't been possible before." But first "we must design systems that will help people overcome the cultural barriers to communication."

NEW KINDS OF TEXTBOOKS?

In the earliest universities, before printing was invented, the lecture was necessary so that the learning of the instructor could be transferred to the minds (or notes) of the learner. Then when printing was invented, the lecturer began to publish, making his work available to a wider audience. Ideally his lectures the next year did not repeat what the students could read in his book but instead updated and enlarged his thought in response to criticisms by other scholars. The time formerly required to cover the basic content of a subject area could then be given to seminars, to discussion and debate with students, to tutoring and guiding the reading of students, and to reading and responding to the writing of students. Now a teacher/author can conduct such a seminar with learners in many countries and with a philosophy of sharing and learning together, not just transferring knowledge.

The success of on-line and TV courses will to some extent depend on the quality and availability of electronic and multimedia textbooks especially designed for or adaptable to differing cultures. We are talking about something different from the vast amount of data available in data bases and libraries. Software and electronic textbooks are needed to manage the overload.

As the textbook of printed lectures and programmed instruction changed the style of teaching and classroom procedures, now the computer and new kinds of multimedia textbooks are beginning to make even greater changes, especially for the distance learner. The phrase electronic publishing can mean several different things, including the communication of information electronically via unused TV channels in the middle of the night or via computer network, for recording at home or school; the automated production of printed materials; and/or the replacement of printed materials with textbooks on diskette, videocassette, CD-ROM, or the cheap plastic "credit card-type Laser disks" that can now contain an entire book. An electronic textbook could provide the student with immediate definitions of words or concepts as needed, with moving picture illustrations, and could replay an illustrated lecture over and over as necessary. Textbooks, available on videodisc for interactive "hypertext" study, could continually grow and change and could individualize and enrich education at all levels (see Sony's "Data Discman.")

One reader who was asked to critique this chapter asks: where is the ombudsman, the Ralph Nader of the electronic textbook? Can an opposition/critic be built into every instructional system from the design stage?

Some publishers already offer to create "tailored textbooks," designed for the particular course of a specific instructor, including different readings and resource materials that the particular teacher requests and assigns. Other publishers offer teaching "packages," which can be on discs or can be sent to students via electronic mail. Such textbook packages may include lectures, demonstrations and homework projects, graphics, animation, sounds, lecture notes, laboratory experiments or projects, and exams. Columbia University's Scholarly Information Center (SIC) developed an on-line political science textbook that was available to students at no cost over the campus computer network (Arms 1990). It is now possible for such a textbook to be available on-line immediately to any overseas student registering through the ConnectEd program of the New School for Social Research. Students can print out sections wherever text on paper is needed. They can use text in more ways than in a bound book because, for example, electronic textbooks can include built-in electronic tutoring and study suggestions in layer under layer of footnotes as well as be automatically searchable for an idea or to trace combinations of ideas.

The extent to which sophisticated and complicated multimedia and interactive electronic textbooks can be accessed by telephone depends on the bandwidth of cables and speed of networks. What is available to Boston or Tokyo via fiber optic cable, therefore, may not for a long time be available in northern Vermont, and for a longer time in rural Bolivia or the Philippines. A textbook on videotape, however, can be sent via satellite to any location in the world, using compression video technology developed by Explore Technology, Inc., (Reitman 1991) to transmit a two-hour movie in 15 seconds (see chapter 11). TV/VCR sets already exist that can print out text from such videos if that is desired.

END OF THE TRADITIONAL TEXTBOOK?

Books, of course, will not disappear. They are too convenient for reading on the bus, while lying in the hammock, or while waiting in line. And there will be new technologies for mass production of books at less cost. For example, many of the costs of producing a printed book, such as storage and shipping, can be eliminated if a bookstore can print a book on demand by connecting to the master copy at the wholesalers or from a diskette.

In any case, however, textbook materials are now available on-line in more remote locations than one would imagine. And such materials are found to be "dynamic and modifiable, much more under the learner's control" (Harasim 1990) than conventional printed materials; indeed the term "textbook" can hardly be used to describe such an integration of text, graphics, software, and on-line resources. An electronic instructional package can be much more flexible for adapting to different cultural and instructional situations, and therefore need not be "watered down to the least common denominator," as is often the case with printed books that are limited by lack of space (see Bolter 1991). Many terms are now used for electronic "packages" that increasingly replace textbooks, for example, the "thoughtbox" linked to a scholar's network (Harasim 1990).

The quality of an electronic book can also be continually improved through being regularly updated with the latest information, research, and feedback from users, both students and teachers. Rather than being discarded after use, it can continually grow in quality as the users become partners in the process of continuing evaluation and feedback. Much of this feedback could be automatically built into the process so that extra time for evaluation of materials is not required of the users. Electronic materials could themselves keep a record of how they are used. For example, a computer/videodisc system can keep a record of a student's successes and failures, tracking student progress and recording feedback (Thorkildsen and Friedman 1984).

Some teaching/research materials being developed for medical education provide a model for improving the quality of electronic teaching materials in other fields. Jerome Glenn (1989) of the United Nations University, which seeks to bring enhanced quality into the research of developing nations, suggests new partnerships between industry and university in the quest for excellence in teaching materials. Most textbooks are now produced by publishing firms in cooperation with teacher/researchers who prepare the text. If high-quality electronic materials can be produced in much larger quantity—for a billion students, Glenn suggests—then there can be enough profit, even if sold at very low cost, to make them available to even the poorest students. (If not, they probably will be pirated as videotapes are.) A learner anywhere in the world might use (rent via an educational electronic "utility") an algebra text/instructional package "designed by the three leading mathematicians, several logicians, and a learning theory analyst." Any student could, according to Glenn's calculations, thus have access to what the very best minds in the world have to offer—for a few cents.

There is no shortage of ideas for electronic textbooks, for either the technology or the contents, as seen in technology such as that reported by Tom Yager (1991) and Elizabeth Greenwood (1991, who reports on "integrated learning systems"). Arthur C. Clarke proposed to UNESCO the development of an "electronic tutor," mass-produced so that the cost would be only a few dollars a year to the student, to help "developing countries leapfrog to the most advanced educational concepts" (Pelton 1990). Nelson Heller (1991b) reports a videodisc system that teachers can use to make customized texts and describes an electronic multimedia textbook in which 150 print pages are embodied so that a user can interrupt any video to get references to related material elsewhere on the disc.

Richard Brandt (1991) reminds us that school closets are stuffed with the wonder boxes of yesteryear and, with illustrations, shows that if technology for education is to survive and be widely used, it must be that which is available to and easily used in the home (like telephones, TVs and VCRs). The director of the "Highly Interactive Computing Environments Group" at the University of Michigan has concluded that "connecting home, school and workplace" is a key to lifelong learning, and that this will happen when hand-held computers become as common and affordable as pocket calculators. This will occur, he believes, once "the price of a lightweight notebook computer drops to around three hundred dollars, and the cost of connecting to an online network falls to about one third of a cent per minute" (Heller 1990).

FROM THE DYNABOOK TO LAPTOP COMPUTER

In the 1970s Alan Kay began working on the "Dynabook" at the Xerox Corporation's Palo Alto Research Center (PARC). He wanted a notebook-sized instrument that could store and retrieve thousands of pages of reference material and that could process animation and play musical scores as well as do accounting (Markoff 1989a). Desktop (and now laptop) computers, which are often called "interim dynabooks," are among the results of Kay's work. His work also has been the foundation for the plan of the Apple Computer Corporation to develop its "Knowledge Navigator," which is to be a book-shaped personal assistant. No one yet knows what its final shape and capacities will be, but developments at the MIT Media Lab and elsewhere (Brand 1987; Cert 1991) provide evidence that all teachers and educators should now begin to prepare themselves to use new forms of textbooks that will play a major role in the coming transformation of all education.

Building on ideas developed at Xerox PARC, Joseph Deken (1981) proposed transforming the linear book into an "electronic tutor" so flexible that readers could change the order of the chapters, reorganizing the material around their own needs and interests. This could provide for interactive and individualized instruction programs and also for more effective styles of study and learning to "break out of the classroom mode" so that learning can be seen as an invitation to explore (also see Bolter 1991).

One planning group (Young et al. 1988) proposes that now is the time to prepare for and develop "the Tablet," the student's personal notebook for the year 2000. The "cover" of the notebook is a touchscreen that looks like the screen on laptop computers. The user could write on it with an electric pen to give it instructions or to store notes in its memory and would be able to insert optical memory laser cards into it with software programs and instructions, one card holding four hours of video or the contents of two thousand books, all for twenty-five cents. For example, Drexler's LaserCard, with a technology similar to much larger videodisc and CD-ROM systems, is already being used for personal medical and insurance records. One card, holding a thousand pages of information, could be reproduced in small or very large quantities and could be regularly updated.

In its more expensive versions, some of these kinds of electronic textbooks could connect to distant data bases via radio or telephone to receive graphics and video as well as text (see Young et al. 1988). Like other instruments there could be inexpensive and very sophisticated versions. The latter could include music and films and keep track of a student's work and monitor progress so as to pinpoint places where the weakness of the learner indicates that extra work is needed.

Many prototypes of such textbooks are now appearing, such as PERSEUS, developed at Harvard for teaching about ancient Greece (Crane 1990); Project EMPEROR which brought together a comprehensive introduction to Chinese art (Ching-chih Chen 1989); and the "Shakespeare Project" (Friedlander 1988) and other programs for simulating the alternatives for studying and staging a drama. Kathleen Wilson's *Palenque* (or "Voyage of Mimi II"), developed at Bank Street School of Education, equally fascinates Ph.D. students and kindergarteners as it teaches anthropology, archeology, geography, flora and fauna; compares ancient Mayan and modern math; and explores ruins, jungles, and museums. Learners, whether children or graduate students, can explore their own interests at their own level of understanding. Such electronic textbooks have the inherent power to provide detailed information for study, to supplement still images and text with motion and sound, and "to present complex kinds of information as clearly and efficiently as the evening news" (Crane 1990). Using images and maps, the scholar using PERSEUS can visit the ancient world ("virtual travel"), tour various sites and pursue the concerns of a historian, linguist, archeologist, philosopher, theologian, anthropologist, or sociologist. Years will pass, Gregory Crane says, before all the major implications of such an electronic textbook can be grasped; but those today who assume that study and research in the future will not be very different from the methods used today, Crane says and demonstrates, need to "reexamine and deepen our own understanding of what we are doing and why."

Multimedia textbooks are being developed in nearly every discipline; for example, in chemistry (Weyh and Crook 1988), in art (*NeXT on Campus* 1991), in-flight training (Murray and Auster 1990), and especially in education by each year's Higher Education software prize winners at EDUCOM. Exciting and effective as many of these electronic textbooks are, by the time a satellite dish is the size of a dinner plate and the receiver/sender is the size of a cigarette pack (Koenenn 1989), they will be seen to have been only primitive first efforts. Alvin Toffler defines a book as "a technology for delivering information and imagery" (Koenenn 1989). Lecturing to a chapter of PEN (the writers' association) about the techno-book, he reported that a device for automatic language translation has already been demonstrated in Japan and said that the marriage of book and computer can enable automatic translation itself into the language of the reader. Another speaker, Paul Soffo of Xerox PARC (also Koenenn 1989), reminded the writers' group that the first book printed in Europe with moveable type "was not welcomed by scholars." Though "a technological *tour de force* it was hard to read [and] lacked page numbers and other features that had to be developed before it became widely used." The textbook with electronic screen, still hard to read, must also greatly improve in quality before it can become popular.

The emerging electronic book not only combines book and computer, but also interactive television. The twentieth century has seen decades of experimentation with radio and television, beginning with a fascination with the technology and resulting in its use largely for entertainment. The serious educational and artistic uses of radio and TV lie in the future as TV and computer merge. Entertainment, news, and sports will continue, but with 150 channels available (Gilder 1990 says a thousand channels on optic cables), new types of educational packages, as yet hardly conceived, can also be used in and from every home, office, or school.

MODEST BEGINNINGS FOR DEVELOPING NATIONS

For the emerging electronic university to succeed, equal attention and imagination must be given to creating and mass producing low-cost appropriate educational technology for learners in underdeveloped parts of the world. Does that mean expensive electronic multimedia books and encyclopedias? Ultimately, yes. But in both rich and poor countries the transition begins with more simple electronic tools for the distance learner.

Electronic textbooks can be transmitted to students and faculty in a variety of ways. For example, the content of textbooks with the most up-to-date information can be downloaded from TV stations or satellite at night, at first perhaps only to a regional center for the use of teachers, next to teachers in the classroom and in time to the electronic slates or notebooks of students themselves. Money now used to buy large numbers of textbooks can be used to pay for the downloading of digital information even to battery-operated TVs—for recording on digital videotape at each school or regional cooperative software loan center.

British Book News, February 1991, reports on the gradual emergence of a global "tele-ordering" system with electronic on-line catalogs and regularly updated CD-ROM catalogs, such as Whitaker's United Kingdom data base of 500,000 books in print. Yet what good is a system that tantalizes African students with what is available, if they cannot afford to order any of it? British publishers, in cooperation with their government, have made an effort to provide low-cost textbooks for countries in Africa and South Asia. Grants to college libraries have made possible book loan centers with 500 copies of certain crucial textbooks (Van Hasselt 1991).

However, advances in medicine, for example, come so quickly that even North American students complain that their medical school textbooks are often soon out of date. In the Third World information may be even more outdated because it takes time for it to be translated into another language. In any case, books are soon worn out and money is often not available to replace them, and just one of the many textbooks an African student needs can cost as much as his family's income for an entire month. Pirated publishing is very common; that is, one copy is bought and then photocopies of crucial pages are shared. But even a photocopy of a hundred pages may cost a student her food money for a week.

So what technology can poor students rent or borrow to use electronic textbook material? We have already suggested that until the electronic university's resources can come to all via TV and/or computer conference, much of it can be made available on a chip costing a few cents, or on LaserCards costing twenty-five cents each. Like the technology needed for the electronic book or tablet, such cards and software can be manufactured in Third World countries at costs that will make it possible for learners there to have better access to the knowledge they need.

Foreign aid and other funds now used to provide extra copies of printed books might in many cases be used to provide electronic equipment to be distributed by college bookstores, which can be similar to shops that rent tools for temporary use. An innovative proposal is being explored and developed by entrepreneur Jack Taub—an "educational utility" (like the telephone company) to distribute electronic courseware. He would finance the distribution of knowledge in the same way that the telephone system has been financed—to use his words, "paid for by users (individuals or schools), five cents for each call." Taub's idea of a "utility" that would make available, on demand, at a modest per-use fee, all the best educational software and information is suggestive of other ways a global system for the distribution of knowledge can be affordable. In 1991 the utility was being experimentally demonstrated in Phoenix, Arizona, as "an educational utility that could transfer the contents of textbooks overnight."

A NEW KIND OF THIRD WORLD SHELL/SLATE?

One traditional way in which pupils functioned without expensive books and paper has been to use erasable blackboards and slates. A slate on their knees, like the teacher's blackboard, can be erased and used over and over. So the first form of electronic book for developing countries might be envisaged as an "electronic shell/slate"—a simple and affordable window on the world (Feldman 1991) on every learner's lap. We are using the word "slate" here to refer to more than the copyrighted "electronic slate" or lap board that can receive and read what a distant teacher writes and transmit to the teacher what a pupil writes.

The word "shell" suggests an electronic container that can be refilled over and over and also a computer program that can be filled in and changed by a teacher. A battery-powered shell/slate could be "erased" and used again and again. A vast amount of information could be stored on inexpensive computer chips or credit-card-sized inserts kept at a regional center; and it need never get out of date because the content can be replaced each week or when a course or study unit is completed. So like the traditional slate, it can be erased and used over and over, where paper and books are used up. It could contain "slots" to which more and more sophisticated technology and connections can be added as they become available and affordable.

Richard Curtis (1991) reports that the cyberbook, "the sharp edge of a technological revolution whose profundity has scarcely been measured, is now being produced." Sony, he says, is already producing the Data Discman at the rate of 20,000 a month. These small CD-ROM players now contain massive reference books (an entire encyclopedia using one-fifth of a disc). Easy for untutored users, these discs can soon include all that is needed for an entire course with sound, music, and animation to make them more useful and interesting. "Over the last few years," Curtis points out, "inventors, engineers, and scientists have conquered obstacle after obstacle." State-of-the-art hypertext makes it possible for users to navigate from one topic to another and to access whole libraries of information. The descendants of the "discman" are already available at a fraction of the price of desktop computers. (Recommended reading: Bolter 1991 describes electronic textbooks and how, as the printing press did, they are beginning to work major changes in culture and learning. Watkins 1991a reports on electronic workstations and textbooks.)

The next chapter tells how a "global electronic student" can find courses and function from a distance.

Ten

THE GLOBAL STUDENT

Students can access their own records via an Automated Teller Machine . : . which dispenses displays and printed reports of personal, academic, and financial information. . . . ASSIST analyzes the student's . . . college transcript and . . . graduation requirements . . . then produces a list of courses to be taken . . . in minutes as opposed to hours of wading through catalogs.

Jane Ryland 1990

For another perspective on the networking university we can look at what is happening through the eyes of students in North America, Asia, and Latin America. How do they get involved in country-to-country electronic education? Some learners, still a privileged few, already take courses from another continent. As is often true of pioneers who blaze the way for multitudes who will follow, these students sometimes find it hard going. They are already moving outside their own nation and culture, beginning to explore a world of courses and galaxies of information.

It is important, however, not to confuse the *electronic* student who is learning to use powerful computer tools on campus with the *global* student who is taking a course from another country, or who is engaged in a research project involving students and faculty in other countries, or whose on-campus course involves an electronic connection with a lecturer, class, or materials from another continent.

Since there is not yet a global catalog, students who would take a course other than through a college where they are registered may explore possibilities by posting a message on a computer bulletin board, asking for information about overseas colleges that offer the specific course needed. At present this tends to be dependent upon serendipity. A student may not find out about a course that would be just right. Or someone in India may reply on-line: "*Byte* magazine (Meeks 1987) says that you can take an MBA or four kinds of undergraduate degrees on the Electronic University network, or that Thomas Edison State College in New Jersey offers courses that can be taken anywhere and has students in seventy foreign countries." Students are not required to travel to the Thomas Edison campus to earn a degree. A student wishing information can get in touch with its CALL computer network. Through it anyone with an IBM compatible computer and modem can search the catalog for possible courses, as well as communicate with advisors or get other information.

The beginnings of an on-line global catalog of courses are seen at the International Center for Distance Learning (ICDL), a documentation center of the British Open University. It has an internationally accessible computer database of subjects available, media used, entrance requirements, and information on specific courses offered electronically by Commonwealth institutions. (Also see Paulsen 1991a, 1991b, and Walker 1990 about a computerized data base, ECCTIS 1000, which provides descriptions and registration information on 60,000 courses.) As a global electronic catalog of offerings available from country to country is created, each university and each nation will discover what it has to give and what it needs to receive in and from a global education network. A student in Europe can now explore on-line the course offerings and available funding for courses in some other countries.

It has been suggested that an on-line catalog might be regularly updated like the computerized telephone directories in France. It is more likely that such a directory of courses and personnel will be "distributed," that is, a section of it will be kept on computers in each country. Again, one model might be the way the American telephone system refers information seekers to a distributed on-line directory. More than seventy higher education institutions are experimenting with a "white pages" directory on Internet, a sort of "world-wide online phone book." Pat McGregor (1991) describes the technology used for "a worldwide, online, interconnected Directory with all sorts of information."

More specific ideas about how to develop and maintain an on-line "distributed" catalog and directory can be found each month in *Boardwatch: Electronic BBS and Online Information Services*, a magazine about electronic bulletin boards. The May 1991 issue, for example, lists phone numbers in the USSR to exchange information about educating the handicapped. (Also see Frey and Adams 1990; Applegate 1991.)

The ARCHIE program at McGill University in Canada can be asked to search through Internet worldwide for information. Such systems may mean that it will not be necessary to employ staff to gather all the world's course information, a never-ending and overwhelming task. Instead, a student looking for a needed course, or a university looking for electronic resources, will be able to use something like ARCHIE to search the on-line catalogs of nearly all the educational institutions in the world. (See Cerf 1991 on "knowbots" and Weinstein and Shumate 1989 on the "smart searcher," which allows a workstation to search and evaluate alternatives.)

HOW STUDENTS STUDY AND LEARN ON-LINE

Present trends suggest that many students will get their education on three campuses: a *residential college* community, whether for a summer or for four years, for guidance, support, evaluation, and motivation; a global *electronic campus* that they can enter via a computer terminal or workstation, "commuting" from home or dormitory room; and the continuing education and training provided *at their workplace* by employers and community organizations. In any case, across a lifetime some courses will be taken on campus, some at home via computer conference or TV, and an increasingly large number of students are likely at one time or another to take courses in a variety of modes.

At the British Open University a student in the 1980s might have spent 80 percent of study time with printed materials that came through the mail (Mason and Kaye 1990); 10 percent of time with audiovisual media, cassettes, and broadcasts; and 10 percent interacting with other students via the telephone, computer conference, and occasional face-to-face meetings. Or students have often used videotapes or audio-taped lectures and discussions, or films such as those that are available to American students over the Public Broadcasting System. In this way a student could meet experts from around the world, travel in space, or journey to the center of a volcano, all without leaving home.

Via a computer terminal, some distance students can now have access to a wider variety of materials and resources than on-campus students do. Distance students, like University of Southern California students now, will be able to consult a computer terminal to find out where they can buy a needed book, for a directory to data bases, and to get access to the vast resources on Internet (Turner 1990b).

Most adult professionals who take an on-line course to get needed skills or information generally study independently without a great deal of help. On the other hand, Robin Mason and Anthony Kaye (1990) point out that undergraduates, such as the distance education students of the New York School of Technology, were often found to need an on-line tutor for support. Electronic students at the University of Guelph were much less likely to drop out if they were given adequate orientation and training. And as is true in face-to-face teaching, a nurturing relationship between instructor and student is also found to be important. After all, students who are residents on campus may also become so dissatisfied with their classroom experience that they drop out of school; therefore, unmotivated on-line students should not be compared with highly motivated on-campus students.

Thomas Edison College's guided study students, working wherever they may be, have been provided with access to an *advisor* who provides regular feedback on written assignments; and to a *mentor*, an expert in that field who is available to answer questions by telephone or on-line. The time undergraduates actually spend on-line could be as low as 5 percent.

The Electronic Learning Network (ELN) at first delivered courses on a computer disc, which included instructions, assignments, and projects, with "an element of telecommunications thrown in to make it more convenient" (Meeks 1987). Then the ELN developed a software system based on the radical change that is transforming higher education: instead of a course centering on an instructor (as when the student came to a class on campus), the instruction revolved around the needs and convenience of the student. The software provided to the student operated on one-key commands. If a student wanted to ask a question, pose a problem, or send a note or assignment to the instructor, he would "hit one [computer] key and the message [would be] automatically delivered" (Meeks 1987). Course assignments were sent to the student in the same uncomplicated way.

The technology for education exchange from country to country can thus be simplified. The student in Singapore who registers for a ConnectEd course in New York City, for example, once she has a modem, simply dials to connect her computer to a mainframe computer in the United States—not much more difficult than making an international phone call. Her software system records the procedure so that it can easily be repeated every day. Once she has dialed to connect with the computer in America, everything is simple and clearly explained. She can read lectures, read comments and papers by other students in the course, ask questions of the instructor, and carry on discussions with other students, simply by typing and receiving messages on her computer terminal. Students on different continents can thus come to know each other personally and work together.

The technology actually used will vary according to the needs of students—their disabilities, for example, or their language capabilities or their course obligations. Instructors may require that examinations and term papers be submitted by fax. A laboratory course may require interactive videodiscs. An anthropology course may provide videotapes of other cultures. A seminar may require more face-to-face personal meetings and encounters on slow-scan TV in addition to continuing on-line discussion.

Michael Moore and G. Christopher Clark (1989a, 1989b) find that by being required to rely on their own resources, on-line students can become self-directed, autonomous learners capable of guiding their own studies throughout life. They learn to call upon a wide variety of learning resources that stretch well beyond the program of the institution delivering the instruction. The global electronic student can at the same time have a more personalized education, tailored to particular needs and interests.

Joseph Pelton (1990), illustrating with the imaginative computerized teaching instruments of David Hon and Project Athena at MIT, sees the evolution of "a new type of community of scholars," which will both replace and supplement the work of today's classrooms. Students can become partners in an enterprise that will greatly enrich their lives and learning (see Dertouzos 1991).

A COURSE ONE'S COLLEGE DOES NOT OFFER

The student taking a course via TV or computer conference may be living on the campus of a college that does not offer what is needed. Indeed, for an indefinite future most students taking courses electronically may be resident students on another campus. In this case, the college itself can help the student find the needed course. For example, Gerd Gast (1991) describes the experience of a student in Australia who took a course, with the help of her college, from Cerritos College in California. She was sent the student handbook from the California college via electronic mail. It explained how to use the CompuServe computer network, a commercial service available in most of the world, and the kind of computer and software she would need to take a course. The California college offered reasonable tuition charges and credit that could be transferred.

With the help of her advisor in Australia, she took the course via the Internet computer network at much less cost. This was possible because the easy-to-use PEGASUS system in Australia makes available to every on-line student a rich variety of services, plus international computer network connections to Brazil, many European countries, the Caribbean, Russia, Japan, and Southeast Asian countries as well as North America.

She had almost no previous experience in using computers, so first she had to master some word processing and file transfer skills. She did so and, at the end of the course, she was rated "the best of her class" of twenty on-line students. Further, the Australian student found her relationship to the instructor in California "to be intimate and supportive," in contrast to the isolation and depersonalization students have experienced in other kinds of distance education (Gast 1991).

TODAY'S ELECTRONIC STUDENTS

Those now taking courses from another country tend to be professionals in need of continuing education or adventurous graduate students who take their "portable work stations" with them wherever they go.

Dale Parnell (1990), the chief executive officer of the American Association of Community and Junior Colleges, foresees transformational cooperation among colleges to enlarge the educational experience of those who are not now well served by higher education: ethnic groups, minorities, the unemployed, scattered rural people, people limited by physical handicaps, older illiterates, prisoners, etc. On the other hand, the students in Paul Levinson's (1988) ConnectEd class on "Popular Culture and the Media" included a marketing writer at a computer corporation, a Yugoslav film editor, an employee of an international child sponsorship agency assigned to establish computer connections to other countries, a video production teacher at a community college, a musician/drummer, and an artists' representative.

The students who take on-line courses, in whatever country, are initially not the typical older adolescent who spends four years on a residential campus. They tend to be older and self-disciplined and are likely to have good verbal skills (see Dille and Mezack 1991). Researchers funded by the Annenberg CPB Project (Brey and Grigsby 1984) found that more than half of the students enrolled in telecourses already had some college education and eight out of ten were seeking to complete or accelerate undergraduate education. Two-thirds were female, perhaps many of them wanting to take their courses at home because they had small children and could not find or afford adequate child care. Less than a quarter of them were traditional college age, and half were thirty or older. Eight out of ten did all their classwork and study at home. Two-thirds were married or divorced; half had at least one dependent.

While an increasing proportion of electronic students in industrial countries were senior citizens and retired persons who had discretionary income and wished to enrich their lives, nearly nine out of ten enrollees were employed. They enrolled because their work schedules conflicted with on-campus courses. Many were in job-related education, possibly reflecting what employers were willing to pay for. Increasing numbers of adults felt pressure to update their job skills to keep their jobs or get better ones. Others wanted to enhance their job potential by retraining for a new career.

Takeshi Utsumi of the GLOSAS/GU project sees the sharing of courses overseas as a great asset for the emerging global business society (also see Glenn 1989). Students can take overseas courses to prepare for jobs in other countries, or for jobs they can do at home while connected electronically with employers in other countries.

THE DISABLED STUDENT

Remarkable computer tools are bringing the whole world of learning into the rooms of paralyzed persons who can hardly leave their beds. Such tools as speech synthesis technology can also help isolated and impaired persons get education through on-line courses. (Yarrish 1991 finds that an instructor interacts on-line with students based on their energy and ideas and without any prejudices "caused by preconceived ideas about skin color, age, body shape or mode of address.") Norman Coombs (1989) reported that one of the first term papers submitted to him was from a hearing-impaired student who had found that she could "talk" better with instructors on-line. A TV lecture, with text/translation and/or captions for the hearing-impaired helps second-language students as well. This has also been found to be true for students with many other kinds of disabilities (Turoff and Hiltz 1988).

Ten percent of American students have disabilities, and America is not worse off than the rest of the world. California community colleges (Kramer et al. 1989) have collaborated to develop a center to provide state-of-the-art technology to enable students with disabilities to participate fully in higher education. Similarly, isolated students with handicaps, anywhere in the world, could also be connected to such tools as the "Assistive Device Interface Selector." It has been developed at the University of California, Berkeley, to help disabled students find the software and devices to make it possible for them to get the same education available to anyone else (also see *Chronicle of Higher Education*, Apr. 16, 1990; and *Educom Review*, Spring 1989, for other projects that provide equal access to disabled students.)

INSTRUCTOR'S ACQUAINTANCE WITH DISTANT STUDENTS

A question frequently raised by critics of TV and on-line courses is: "How can an instructor really get well-enough acquainted with a student who is perhaps thousands of miles away?" Several new and emerging types of software can radically change the teacher/learner relationship and enlarge the opportunity for an instructor to know any such student at greater depth. These are study-management software; the student's personal studystation/workstation; software for construction of a personal data base; and the creation of a unique profile of each student that can help both distant students and faculty in the process of personal acquaintance.

Study-Management Software

Study-management software can be used to help learners to organize their work, to establish a personal discipline for self-directed study, to set short-term and long-range goals, to plan each day's work as part of a month-long or semester plan, and to facilitate the completion of each task and master each skill on schedule. By monitoring this process of helping students plan their study, each instructor can learn more about students than has generally been the case in personal interviews and conversation.

For example, "Project Jefferson" (Chignell and Lacy 1988) provides an "integrated electronic notebook" that brings together various kinds of computer tools to empower students in their regular work and study. On each assignment it prods and reminds students, using focus questions to help them organize each assignment. It also supplies background information, sources, and a place to add personal ideas. It uses hypermedia, which "along with other technology is leading to a vision of a global information system" for navigation through a body of knowledge, with browsing tools, authoring tools, and other guides for the student. The notebook can gradually be enlarged and extended to bring in information developed for other courses. It will be used for various types of research, for example, as an anthropology field research tool. As it is tested at the University of Southern California, "it will be linked to a global library system." Indeed, its authors suggest that the library of the future may be build around such learning tools, rather than the student's tools being adapted to the present types of libraries.

The Electronic Desk or Studystation

The term workstation is often used for special combinations of tools brought together for effective use by students and teachers. This term, however, is more properly used for powerful personal computing devices in engineering and science (Arms 1990). So a different term is needed for a combination of software tools for students in other disciplines, to bring together all needed technology in a form that is also easy for distance students to use. An electronic desk might include a talking helmet for immersion in foreign language study. (See Arms 1990 for some University of Illinois components.) To avoid confusion, I will use the term studystation for students not in engineering or science.

The technological package that is possible now for students in North America, Europe, and Japan can bring together many more kinds of software and capabilities than the "shell/slate" proposed for students in countries with more limited communication facilities and financial resources. If there could be international agreement among countries on what the ultimate studystation for the on-line or TV students should be like, it could be mass-produced with adaptations to include what is needed for different fields of study, for example, searchable reference books, music composition software, or procedures for scientific experiments. Such a studystation can be tailored to the unique needs and interests of the individual student as well as to a particular course or discipline.

A Personal Knowledge Base

Another software component of a studystation can integrate all of the previous work done by a student, systematically organizing it. Instructors have always learned more about each student through reading each term paper, exam, and other assignments. Now studystation software can make this process cumulative as each new study project is added to and becomes part of what some call the student's enlarging "knowledge construct" (Wojciechowski 1986). All students can keep a computer record of every significant book and article they read, not only a bibliography but also their reading notes and their own personal ideas suggested by that reading. Studystations can be used then at any time to search through all that one has written or read, by author, title, or subject, or from word indexes and cross-indexes organized around current study projects and/or long-range interests and needs.

All the information that students record can thus be preserved in three ways:

- as the lecturer or electronic textbook presents and organizes it;
- as learners reorganize the material in their own notes, as a way to understand it;
- and as the student's studystation software automatically places various kinds of information where it belongs in that learner's "body of organized knowledge."

Already the use of word processing in preparing term papers and research reports makes it possible for software programs to add all of such creative and scholarly work to the learner's personal knowledge base automatically. The written work can be preserved in its original form and at the same time can be taken apart or indexed so that ideas and information can also be deposited automatically along with a learner's other information on the same topic, according to the personal knowledge base index. Each new paper or project can thus build upon, improve, and enlarge existing papers and knowledge-base sections.

The studystation can be responsive to each learner's particular strengths, weaknesses, talents, and needs as the studystation also studies the learner as he or she uses it, adding to the computerized profile of the learner, which develops and enlarges as a student interacts with it.

A studystation could also make it easy for students to locate learners with similar research interests at home or abroad. This could help create "communities" of students—connected electronically across national borders—who are interested in working on a particular project. The studystation can make possible a new pedagogy in which students assume responsibility for managing their own learning, scheduling, evaluating, and reviewing so as to better organize and master their courses. Enlarged motivation also comes with success, for example, by providing tutoring when it is needed by continuing personal contact with an online instructor.

Perhaps the most important contribution of the worldwide electronic university system to the individual student can be studystation tutoring. The studystation could include a tutoring component to keep track of the interactions between the student and the tutoring system, as well as expert systems to pull together all information needed to counsel a learner (and family) on needs and progress, and to tailor an educational program to meet a student's unique needs. Howard Gardner (1983) calls this a "profile."

A Computerized Profile of Each Student

All this assumes, however, that each student's studystation will help create and maintain a "computerized profile," a comprehensive and confidential record which may be kept on a "smart card," such as those used for storing large amounts of medical history information (see Smart Card 1991). The profile can include an overview of needs, problems, goals, opportunities, talents, and gifts. It may begin with diagnosis and expand like the physician's comprehensive medical record. It might include a continually enlarging model of the individual's kinds of intelligences (Gardner 1983) and learning styles. Eleanor Smith (1987) suggests using an electroencephalogram and Jon Franklin (1987) reported how scientists at the University of Texas Health Science Center in Dallas, using a scanner similar to the PET, discovered highly individualistic brain patterns that could help "monitor the progress of students and suggest to professors which points should be covered next."

Education plans and programs founded on such a software-managed computer profile of each person may at present seem a remote possibility for distance students, especially those in the Third World. Once the process is developed and the needed technologies are mass-produced for the industrialized nations, however, the software can then become available at reasonable cost to the rest of the world also. (Pilot experimentation at Georgia Institute of Technology is reported in Arms 1990.)

At present much of what has been learned in periodic evaluations is lost. Without cross-indexed computerization, there has not been an adequate way for comprehensive information to become the foundation for counseling and for determining further steps in education. With computer-empowered analysis/diagnosis, more sophisticated insights into the needs and potential of each person can be enlarged and enriched plans can be proposed for that person's future.

What about confidentiality? A great deal of information about intellectual, psychological, artistic, and other kinds of growth and development is in fact collected during a learner's lifetime. In its present disorganized, scattered, and poorly managed form it is incomplete and may be abused (see Cookson 1989). Such emerging tools are forcing a fundamental reexamination of the way information about people is coordinated and used in health care, church, government records, and business and insurance as well as in education. Confidentiality of all student records, in a global computer system, must be protected.

On one hand, professional educators must find ways to use pejorative information as carefully as physicians do. This is both possible and essential. In France 130,000 patients have been involved in experimentation to determine how to computerize records without endangering privacy. Each patient's updated "smart card" with all important medical information is the patient's private property, presentable only on a voluntary basis. One way to guarantee that is to program safeguards into the technology. (Gilder 1990 describes cryptology which releases only the permitted information.) Physicians and others who used such records would "have access only to that part of the information necessary" for them to do their jobs "but the carrier of the card could check the entire contents of his file at any time at a public terminal" (Smart Card 1991). Anyone who has a reason to do so should have the right to withhold information, but should also understand that this may significantly weaken the effectiveness of education, much as withholding medical records could serious affect the quality of health care. The technology that many feared would depersonalize education has thus opened up alternative possibilities.

ON-LINE CAMPUS SOCIAL LIFE?

Students are already using computer conferencing and teleconferencing to reach out to students in other countries. One begins to see the emergence of a new kind of electronic global student community. Education by electronic means can never be the same as in a campus face-to-face community, but an on-line global student community may be on the horizon. A "global campus" publication, *Alternatives Journal*, edited by students at Grinnell, was in 1989 on a computer network for students in the United States and abroad (*Chronicle of Higher Education*, May 10 1989). Another such student journal was edited by students in Russia and California (*New York Times*, July 9, 1989).

Even some electronic global social life beings to occur. For example, graduate students in Berkeley had a New Year's party with a group of graduate students in Moscow via the EIES computer network and slow-scan TV. ConnectEd (New School of Social Research in New York) had an electronic Halloween party with participants from Europe and the Middle East and has operated a "coffee house" for informal socializing among students in various countries enrolled in its courses. (See Rasmussen et al. 1991 on socialization on-line among students in sixteen northern European universities.) Edward Yarrish (1991) finds that the socialization processes that take place in the halls and cafeteria for on-campus students can also "be encouraged in the electronic university."

An increasingly significant on-line global student community is seen in international social and political action projects in which students in various countries coordinate their activities through international computer networks—whether to preserve whales, clean up rivers, work for disarmament, or oppose apartheid. Student political activities and a wide variety of international action projects, student discussions, and other "intercollegiate activities" can be found on the PeaceNet computer network. Students in many countries are on-line with each other for such projects much more than is generally realized. Underlying tacit support for such activity is an understanding, expressed by the director of a public policy program at Harvard University who said: "International connectivity . . . is an expression of [student] rights to further their individual interests on a global scale" (Branscomb 1989).

GAINS FOR THE STUDENT

The surprising thing, reported over and over in research (see Moore and Clark 1989a, 1989b), is that electronic instruction—via teleconference and/or computer conference—can be as effective as traditional classroom-based lectures and face-to-face discussions. Comparing the results of courses taught on-line with those at an excellent college, it was found that the use of the computer-empowered technology actually improved the quality of education, involving students more actively in self-teaching as well as in joint study efforts with other students. Many students report that they are in closer touch with their instructors, and often also with other students and are engaged in joint study projects as much as or more than are those who attend regular college classes in person. One student in Hong Kong reported that it was easier for him to confer with an instructor in British Columbia than it was for him to find his instructor in Hong Kong.

Starr Roxanne Hiltz (1990), who has led in researching such questions, finds that on-line students:

- have test scores as good as those in conventional classrooms if the quality of instruction is the same;
- report improved access to instructors and convenient access to needed courses and educational experiences if they have adequate technology to use;
- and tend to develop improved ability to collaborate and communicate with other students.

(For recommended reading on self-directed, individualized, and adult learning and on one's own unique profile, see Gross 1991.)

The next chapter discusses what a global higher education network can mean for continuing education, adult education, and primary and secondary schools in all communities.

Eleven

LIFE-LONG EDUCATION
IN THE COMMUNITY

The day the telegraph was invented, the first reaction of the Pony Express . . . was to try to buy faster horses. Then they tried to hire better riders. They did not realize that the world had changed.
Ray Mabus 1991

To get another perspective on the emerging worldwide university, the planning needed, and the changes it is bringing, this chapter discusses the impact of such a global network on nonuniversity towns and neighborhoods, rich and poor—first, the potential effect on South Africa, and second, its possible impact on a Connecticut county. Can the electronic university show how courses that are not otherwise available can be provided to match the needs and interests of all ages of people in any community? Can the electronic university provide resources and models for county-wide or regional consortia, involving business and industry, to serve the job training and continuing education needs of all citizens?

DEFINING LOCAL EDUCATION IN GLOBAL TERMS

The organizations that are being created to facilitate the emergence of the electronic university are also promoting "cradle-to-grave" education. The electronic university's constituency is not defined merely as four residential undergraduate years plus an elite group of postgraduate students. "The University of the World [relates] to all academic activities from preliterate education through primary, secondary and high school, undergraduate colleges, graduate and professional studies, postdoctoral work, and continuing education. The University hopes to include all blocs of nations and all individual countries" (UW 1991).

Many poorer countries must concentrate their efforts—and need electronic university assistance—in first developing better education for children and for universal literacy, then for secondary schools and job training, and, third, for higher education for leadership and entrepreneurial training to raise the economic level of the community and nation.

The major industrial countries are struggling with how to provide better quality scientific education to equip the population with new skills needed for an information age. "The United States has already become a 'learning society', with close to 40 percent of the population in some organized learning situation all the time" (Newrowe 1988). In urbanized countries where support is eroding for the public schools because parents with children are a declining minority, it is important for education leaders to see that *everyone* in the community must now be their constituency; this means taking seriously the partnership of schools with business and with all of the other educational and training institutions to provide schooling to meet everyone's educational needs.

The Union of South Africa provides an interesting case because, as in the United States, the Third World and First World exist within the country side by side. The report of a two-year study on how "electronic media and modern telecommunication systems could assist . . . South Africa in solving some of the critical problems in [its] educational systems" (Spier 1991) asked how the imaginative application of electronic media can assist in solving these pressing problems:

- a huge population to serve with high population growth, some 50 percent of the black population under fifteen years of age
- shortage of funds for education, resulting in large classes and underqualified teachers, irrelevant syllabi; shortage of infrastructure, teaching materials, laboratories; many schools without electricity
- high dropout rates: only 5 percent graduate from secondary school
- higher education skewed towards academic subjects at the expense of the technical ones (and proper job training)
- universities and technical schools underfunded
- quality of staff not up to international standards
- tuition too expensive for blacks and scholarship funds limited

To meet those problems, a nonprofit "Learning Network Cooperative" (LNC) was proposed to

- train subject experts in designing electronic courseware in a team contest;
- produce such courseware for all subjects where there is a large demand, shortage of teachers, and marketability of the skill or knowledge;
- establish Community Learning Centers equipped with workstations capable of transmitting the courseware;
- and establish Corporate Learning Centers in which employees of business corporations can get courses on a decentralized basis (for example, the NTU model from chapter 2 which the South African report sees as "the most impressive model for tertiary education using electronics").

CONTRIBUTIONS OF A WORLD UNIVERSITY NETWORK

To achieve such goals, the emerging worldwide electronic university can offer:

- models and experience from other countries on what technology can do and not do, possibilities that can encourage a conservative educational bureaucracy (which exists in nearly all countries) to understand and support some experimental changes;
- some demonstrations of how to make electronic education and connections affordable;
- the challenge to move towards a "learning society," which seeks to bring education into every home and enhanced educational opportunities into every school and learning center;
- and a philosophy of self-directed, individualized education that can empower people to create wealth and jobs (so they can pay for better education, homes, health care) and to bring cultural enrichment into all lives and communities.

A review of applicable experience elsewhere suggests that an effort to improve the quality of all education in South Africa also needs to include "blacks and whites all in one school system." Also needed in many such countries is an electronic system to aid a classroom teacher in coping with students who come from homes that speak different languages.

An electronic system could compensate for shortages of teachers and could provide advanced high-quality courses in many schools by connecting talented students with a class at another school that offers what is needed. As in many American schools now, all schools could be equipped with a satellite dish to receive course materials, which could then be downloaded onto videotape so that students could use them over and over.

Starting with what is possible with existing TV, radio, telephone service, and videotape recorders, the cooperative system could then move to install simple two-way technology that can be placed in neighborhood learning/tutoring centers as well as in many homes. Job-training courses might be funded by cooperatives, at least in part by small bank loans to groups of mothers to start small businesses, the profit from such small cooperatives going to improve quality of life and provide funds for education (as is done by the Grameen Bank in Pakistan and the Ecumenical Cooperative Bank, which has its headquarters in Holland).

There is no electricity in homes and schools? The Asian-produced, small, battery-powered TV sets that are everywhere in mountain village bamboo huts in the Philippines and the transistor radios in the hands of the impoverished shepherd on a Middle East desert suggest that inexpensive battery-powered educational instruments can be mass-produced and affordable. (see *The Orbiter* 1990).

THE NEED TO SHARE EXISTING RESOURCES

However, the key to beginning to use communications/computer technology to improve all local education requires some new understanding of and approaches to sharing. The term often suggests that money be taken from well-funded neighborhood schools to be given to impoverished schools. For how else, it is asked, can poor communities develop the quality of education required to raise their economic level so that they can afford good education?

That need changes, however, in the information age. There is a limited amount of money to share, but an unlimited amount of knowledge. Indeed, the more knowledge is shared, the more it increases. More importantly, the new communications/computer technology makes possible some kinds of sharing that can add to the quality of one school without taking away from the quality of the other. And it makes it possible for each school to seek expertise in one specialty and to share that program with other schools in the region.

In 1991, because of huge federal and state deficits and the recession in the local economy, many American states were having to make drastic cuts in school and college budgets. Programs for handicapped students were modified, innovative language programs such as the teaching of Chinese were eliminated from high schools, and job retraining and programs for gifted children were in some cases almost abandoned. How then could eastern Connecticut afford what the President of the United States was calling for in 1991: a drastic retooling of outmoded educational programs and institutions, just as factories have to be retooled for a changing global economy?

In *Setting National Priorities*, Brookings Institution economist Henry Aaron (1990) called for discarding obsolete approaches in education and pointed out that progress can be made without increased funds. Local school officials begin to ask some questions with global (and certainly South African) implications. For instance: if there is less money, then why not spend more of existing funds on electronic sharing?

The beginning of an answer points out that every little school system does not need to try to offer every needed course and program. Satellite dishes are appearing in school yards all over North America and special cable lines are being extended to school buildings (and next to homes) by cable TV and telephone companies. So if there is no money for a high school course in Chinese (in which only a few local students enroll), such a specialized teacher and course can be shared among many schools as is now done in Kansas (see Heller 1991e, 1991f).

As small Pennsylvania rural high schools with limited course offerings give students the opportunity of connecting via telephone-computer-TV to a school that offers any course that is wanted or needed, the same opportunity can be offered to students all over the world. As the best schools in wealthy South African neighborhoods begin to enrich their offerings by such global connections, the same technology can make it possible for them to share this "educational and information wealth" with even the poorest South African schools.

The TI-IN network in the United States, a cooperative satellite venture between private enterprise and public education, offers hundreds of hours of interactive educational programming each week, with regular academic classes, teacher training programs, college credit courses, "basic skill boosters," student enrichment programs, test reviewing and special programs for handicapped students. Such courses are not as yet cost-effective for individual students at home, but do provide economies for school districts. To illustrate: the commissioner of education in Kansas is at work on a project to build regional two-way video learning networks in a partnership with local telephone companies so that electronic sharing can make it possible for eight school districts, none of which could afford a Spanish teacher, to share one who teaches Spanish to all (Heller 1991c).

MUCH BETTER EDUCATION FOR LESS MONEY

To accomplish such sharing, in my opinion, eastern Connecticut needs a county-wide consortium of public and private schools, libraries, adult education programs, business training programs, colleges, and government agencies. Expanding and using some ideas and resources from the consortia involved in the emerging worldwide electronic university, this local cooperative could plan and create all the kinds of education that are needed to serve all ages and needs in the area. Much more technology can be afforded if the various institutions in the consortium share it and cooperate, for example, allowing schools to use business computer networks at night until fiber cables are in place to greatly reduce costs.

This can be an alternative to the often-suggested plan to use buses to take children from neighborhoods with bad schools to schools in rich suburbs. Instead, a kind of "electronic busing/commuting" can make it possible for all children, rich and poor, to participate in the best school programs. Rather than bringing parents of rich and poor schools into conflict, both groups can cooperate from the start in developing electronic programs for the benefit of all. Note how the state of Kansas, to further build "information communities," is planning to form networks of schools, hospitals, universities, and media resource centers (Heller 1991c).

One of the motivations for an eastern Connecticut consortium could be purely economic; that is, the retraining of all workers and the research needed to retool the economy and replace jobs are now being lost as a result of defense funding cuts. Its basic goal could be to provide every citizen with any kind of education that is needed or wanted, on the assumption that democracy and an information-age economy require a citizenry that is continually reeducated.

WHAT CAN BE SHARED AND HOW?

A number of years ago, Yale University abolished a number of its major divisions, including the schools of engineering and education. This was done because it was realized that knowledge and research specializations have increased to the extent that it is no longer possible for any one school or university to offer everything its students and faculty might wish. Each school should therefore do only what it can do with excellence, within the framework of funding and other resources available to it.

The next logical step is for schools and universities to offer to the world whatever they do with excellence (as college faculties have long done by writing textbooks and publishing lectures and research reports) and for students to gain access to courses at other schools and universities that are not offered by their own. Elite students have long migrated to other colleges and other countries to supplement their college work, and that migration now begins to be electronic; therefore, it can become affordable to a majority of students, not just a wealthy elite.

This same logic should now be applied to education at every level. No local school can provide everything, certainly not an African school with limited funds, nor should it try to do so. Local funding and resources should be used to provide what can best be done locally, especially counseling, tutoring, personal attention, and dealing with local needs and issues. For the rest there can be connections to adjacent schools, regional centers, and, where necessary, to the world, providing for primary, secondary, or college education, and for adult and continuing education. The money saved can then be used to help fund the necessary technology.

A suggestive model for such sharing is already provided by many interlibrary loan systems. If a local library does not have a requested book, it turns first to the area consortium of libraries, then to the state library, and to the libraries of universities. This suggests how school systems (certainly the smaller and poorer ones as well as the smaller colleges) can develop consortia, regional centers to share courses, and resources so that each individual can obtain what is needed or wanted.

COOPERATION WITH BUSINESS ILLUSTRATED

An American film corporation is building "multi-media entertainment complexes" in many Third World countries, with "state of the art" digital technology for downloading prize fights or rock concerts as they occur. The latest films can be sent instantaneously from Hollywood or Europe. It was pointed out that this sophisticated satellite computer/TV technology would for the most part be used only evenings and weekends. An actress asked, when visiting South Africa, why not use these complexes also for education through the week?

So the film company, in cooperation with the South African government, is experimenting with calling them education-and-entertainment-complexes with a high priority being given to the use of this sophisticated technology, funded by entertainment, to bring enlarged educational opportunity to underequipped and understaffed schools. An educational foundation has been established, which is also seeking percentages of profit from other film companies. Education space has been offered in the complexes. At first, teachers may be brought to these theaters for training in using technology, and then students can be bused in also. Soon, however, via telephone lines, microwave, or cable TV, schools can be connected to the entertainment centers to receive and send out the very best electronic educational programming available. It is not assumed that this alone can meet South Africa's needs for quality education for all, but it can be an important beginning. As in the American Midwest, excellent instruction in science and math, for example, can be brought into every school room via TV and computers.

State-of-the-art electronic materials, downloaded via satellite onto videotape and laser disc—perhaps on the model of the earlier-described "education utility"—can be made available to even the poorest schools. The goal of the business-financed foundation is to demonstrate how higher quality education can be provided: basic primary education, teacher training, and enrichment programs for secondary schools, colleges and technical, vocational and professional education. When this project succeeds in South Africa, such education/entertainment complexes will also be developed in the USSR, China, Latin America and "in three-fifths of the world." The film company sees its cooperation with the schools as important to the industry because educated people with better jobs will have more money to spend on entertainment.

It has also been suggested that as these new sophisticated kinds of theaters are developed in American inner cities, they can also cooperate with schools to bring higher quality education to Third World areas of the United States as well.

REGIONAL CENTERS

Some American school districts, in order to serve a larger constituency, have set up regional trade schools, sports academies, high schools of science, schools of the performing arts, culinary schools, and schools with many other kinds of specialties, sending students to them by bus. Electronic connections can help them serve many more students and offer much higher quality programs, although some students will continue to be bused to a regional trade school, for example.

Also, many local schools can develop a specialty to share with a larger constituency. One school might specialize in health education, or ecology, or in citizenship education with special electronic connections to all of the agencies of government. One might specialize as a crafts/arts center (including computer art, using new software to enable youngsters to compose music and make films and videos) or become a job preparation center (providing apprenticeship, counseling, job placement). One might become a center for the electronic empowering of the disabled (see Kramer et al. 1989), hospitalized, imprisoned, or homebound students (with on-line courses and tutoring available on a seven-days-a-week basis).

The electronic resources needed by such centers would vary from region to region and country to country. One model is the first "rural tele-service and information center" built in Denmark in 1985; now there are twenty-eight of them in Scandinavia. Some are located in libraries or schools, and some in remodeled houses, whatever is adequate to provide work space for computers, modems, printers, VCRs, fax machines, and a great variety of software. These centers are widely used in communities as small as a thousand people for distance education, information services, teleconferencing, and consultation. Because of the success of these centers in helping enrich and transform rural life, for example, in towns too small to have schools, an Association of Tele-Service Centers has been formed with headquarters in Geneva, Switzerland.

A REGIONAL MEDIA/TECHNOLOGY
RESOURCE CENTER

Especially in poorer countries and Third World districts of American cities or South Africa, the heart of educational retooling may begin with a *regional computer/resource center*. It could rent computers, videodisc players, multi-media textbooks, and software for composing music or making films to students and parents. The regional center probably also should be a school for those of all ages who want courses in the repair of technology, in operating electronic equipment, as well as for those who need to function in a technological society but who do not wish to prepare for a trade. Through electronic connections to universities or centers with the best technology, it could offer much more advanced instruction to prepare young people for the computer/information age. It would purchase, service, and provide all the sophisticated technology that retooled schools are going to need.

There has been a proposal in Oregon for a statewide center that, among other things, would franchise local stores in every community to sell and rent such software and equipment. The store would also provide access on an hourly fee basis—whether for children, business people, or adult study and action groups—to any and all of the world's 10,000 computer networks and hundreds of thousands of data bases on all subjects (also see Ditlea 1990).

This proposes a useful model for making such connections and equipment available in poor communities and countries. Where, for example, it would cost one person ten dollars an hour to connect to global ecology data bases and to rent the equipment for research there, a club of local ecologists could share the cost, ten people at a dollar each, or a hundred people at ten cents each. Teachers and students could thus rent high-quality educational hardware and software—videodiscs and multimedia textbooks—and could access on-line library services, even from distant countries, by paying a low cost per minute.

The Fairfax County, Virginia, public schools are developing a media center, with the active cooperation of business corporations, which will deliver "interactive video programming to classroom-based teacher workstations from a video-disc changer (the 'video jukebox')." The center's first task is training teachers, for example, to use the video encyclopedia—which includes film and video clips of major historical events—and other sophisticated resources. The center's software will make it possible for a teacher to line up segments in advance to be delivered at specific times to a particular class. The center will contain an IBM computer lab; Apple Computer's "20th Century navigator," a Hypercard program that offers students five separate search strategies; and will have the capacity to create its own interactive videodiscs, for example, for language and social studies (Heller 1991b). It is not science fiction to suggest that such facilities and programs can be electronically interconnected for sharing, at first perhaps for poorer schools in South Africa to use at off-hours, until funding is secured for more complete equality in education.

LOCAL/GLOBAL SCIENCE CENTERS

Many people do not yet realize the extent to which school children are already reaching out to the world electronically to enlarge educational opportunities. Many fifth and sixth graders are participating in the National Geographic KIDSNET program that has linked a thousand schools—some as remote as Siberia—through a computer network. The Florida Department of Education now recommends that all schools participate in this "hands-on" project in which the children do real scientific work such as testing their own drinking water and collecting rain samples and conducting tests to discover patterns of acidity in rainwater. The samples sent to government scientists save a great deal of money. How else could scientists so inexpensively collect acid rain samples in so many locations? Also, a half million pupils have taken turns at a computer terminal to participate actively as scientists explored the sea off the coast of Italy. The children engaged in two-way conversation with the scientists, making suggestions for the next exploration. A network of universities can help extend such adventurous science education to all of the children (and adult learners) in the world, electronic connections making it possible for many schools to help fund such projects through paying small per-minute charges.

Many problems now limit the use of telecommunications in schools; these include parents and taxpayers who do not yet see the economies and quality that can result. Teachers also lack skills, administrators often fear change, and many schoolrooms are not equipped with telephone lines, much less optical fiber cable. Most teachers do not even know about K12Net, which "currently links over a hundred electronic bulletin boards across North America, Australia, Europe, and soon the USSR" (Rickard 1991). This global network "provides [teachers with] FREE international communications capabilities with local calling access." It uses FREDmail (Apple computers) and FIDOnet (IBM) which includes ten thousand computer bulletin boards in over fifty countries. On-line are conferences on arts and crafts, business education, health and physical education, language arts, mathematics, music and performing arts, science, talented and gifted education programs and conferences for teacher help and support.

This global sharing among schools of many countries was initiated by teachers. It exists "on a global scale, using existing technology at very low cost" and teachers can start and interconnect a computer bulletin board of their own, "without approval of twelve layers of administration . . . and put it into play globally, and immediately connect to an existing network of other teachers and schools." Seth Itzkan (n.d., 1987) reports how one junior high teacher in Boston, totally on his own initiative and funding, set up a joint connection between his school and one in Japan, the youngsters working together daily for a couple of years.

The Science 2000 project in California, in addition to interactive discs and "hands on manipulation science kits," provides students with a free long-distance 800 number they can use to communicate with other classes via "electronic bulletin boards" (Heller 1991a). Through the New York State Education and Research data communications network (NY-SERNet), secondary school pupils in 1991 have access to the high-speed computing network of the National Science Foundation (NSFNet), and through it to Internet, which has connections to educational and research institutions all over the world.

A major contribution of the electronic university to community schools may in some cases be to provide master teachers and to demonstrate that, at least when necessary, the teacher can be in another town or another country. The technicians who keep the system operating may also be in another town or another country.

Whether we are thinking about America or South Africa, one of the most important contributions of the worldwide electronic university can be in teaching the educators, the school board, school administrators, public officials, teachers, and parents. Adults can set an example, showing how parents can teach their children and also learn with them as everyone gets challenged by home-centered learning opportunities. Motorola Corporation, for example, finding that much of its work force could not read or do simple arithmetic, created "Motorola University" as a new model for education. It has no campus, but is a network of partnerships with schools, community colleges, and universities (Gifford 1991). And over 400,000 people a week, out of a population of 2.5 million, are involved in the Knowledge Network in British Columbia, Canada, which provides public general education for a broad range of interests and age groups (Lundin 1988).

In September 1989, the governor of Kentucky proposed to the President of the United States that there should be a "dedicated education satellite in the public domain" (Heller 1991a). Such a satellite could provide equal access to education, "regardless of the wealth of an individual, school district or state." A six-month study found that 111 suppliers of educational programming were already delivering their products by satellite and that 20 of the larger educational program suppliers planned to purchase over 75,000 hours of satellite time during the 1990–91 school year. This study found that, not including business-televised training, there were over 55,000 "receive sites" in the United States, 16 percent of school districts having satellite dishes.

After examining various technologies that might be used, including coaxial cable and optical fiber networks, the report concluded that the "best means by which to distribute multiple educational programs simultaneously . . . at a relatively low cost" would be a public-access satellite. The report (Heller 1991b) cited the Black Satellite Network and the National Technological University (NTU) in reporting that educational agencies are at a financial disadvantage, "spending much more for their satellite time than if their buying power was aggregated. Costs could be greatly reduced by sharing through buying cooperatives."

To paraphrase Therese Mageau (1991), sharing through the emergence of the worldwide electronic education network can

- inspire and motivate tired teachers;
- be a catalyst for broad reforms in education;
- provide sustained training to help all citizens in implementing new technology successfully;
- and can help equalize opportunity for all students, understanding the centrality of learning as the key to human survival.

(Recommended reading: Gilder 1990 on home study, thousands of educational opportunities on networks, and Stuart and Thomas 1991 on even primary pupils having access to world-class experts.)

The next and last chapter briefly mentions some ideas under consideration by long-range planning committees of the University of the World project and other such agencies and raises some large questions and problems yet to be considered.

Twelve

EDUCATION FOR THE NEXT CENTURY

... where the age of television has bred passive, disengaged students with short attention spans, cyberspace may be able to captivate them and foster their active involvement in their own education, [permitting] collaboration between students from remote locations [and] more fully utiliz[ing] students' brains.

Rory Stuart and John Thomas 1991

Without knowing for sure whether long-range results will be modest or excitingly successful, many groups and creative persons are engaged in imaginative and serious planning for phases of the worldwide electronic university. This survey report has suggested many items for their agenda and raises many unanswered questions. One of the most crucial: can politicians now shift major attention from hardware (satellites, cables, etc.) to the development of creative educational software? And can hyperspace, where this kind of education occurs, be a human place?

The stakes are high. Humanity's very survival may depend on its ability to educate as many as possible of the 6 billion people in the world. The teachers and scientists trained in the universities are crucial. Without better education and research the hungry poor of the earth may drag humanity down to disaster. Without better global higher education, actively involving a much higher percentage of the world's population, we may destroy our ecological system and with it ourselves.

On the other hand, humanity is on the edge of potentially tremendous new possibilities in education and in solving fundamental global problems. University Chancellor Arthur C. Clarke (let us nominate him as honorary chairperson of an ideal planning committee) says in the preface of Joseph Pelton's book, *FutureTalk*, that it is probably true in communications technology that anything we can think of can probably be accomplished if it does not violate natural laws.

Pelton (1990), on the basis of his INTELSAT experience, writes about the "global electronic machine," the huge and to most people almost invisible communications system that is transforming all of human life and institutions. That system makes possible, if not almost inevitable, the development of a worldwide electronic education network for the space age. The technology exists. So the question, as in war and peace, economic justice, and world health, is: how can humanity be motivated to develop and use it properly?

John Markoff (1991) suggests caution about global computer networks, warning that the unexplored "virtual wilderness . . . seems to harbor as many dangers as the rest of society" (such as network vandals, operating in distant corners of the globe, who have made "Internet an unsafe neighborhood in recent years"). So while the informal computer networks ("the commons" for all people) will continue to be useful for experimentation and demonstrations, the worldwide electronic university must use safe, professionally managed systems.

The chairperson of the Federal Communications Commission (Andrews 1991) "sees a world in which people . . . use satellites and high speed fiber-optic communication lines to take college courses at home, have television sets which double as multimedia computer work stations, use communication networks to transmit the contents of an entire library in seconds and track down a person anywhere on the globe to deliver the data." But, he says, this requires governments to overhaul their communications policies, for example, to provide space on crowded airwaves for pocket-sized telephones and two-way interactive television. The political pressures and problems are enormous. A shift in power is opposed by corporations whose profits may be greatly reduced by the competition of new services that can provide great educational opportunities (also see Gilder 1990 on the competition).

An education "sending" system—even as satellite costs are greatly reduced—will not serve the needs of all of humanity, Edmund Andrews says, unless there is now a major emphasis on developing the "receiving" software for every school and home. The coming combination of telephone, TV, computer, satellite-dish receiver, and radio, connected to the world satellite network, can make it possible for the developing countries to bypass all of the interim steps (as they have done in transportation with airplanes) and enter into a global education system at affordable cost.

There are now a billion television sets in homes across the world, Pelton says. When humanity is ready, the TV sets can be replaced by battery- or solar-powered, two-way sender/receivers (combining TV and computer), thus shifting from passive to active mode, from entertainment to new possibilities for education. Different segments of what is needed already exist in one country or another. The French Minitel system in which home telephones have been replaced with computers is one illustration, because it is essential that receivers, in whatever form they are developed, be easy to use and available in homes as well as schools.

VOUCHERS AND ELECTRONIC AID

"Without the latest techniques in electronic schooling," which this hardware now makes possible, Pelton says, "there seems little hope for people even in the United States, much less the rest of the world." Yet how are these electronic receivers, the software, and access to global library systems to be afforded by the poor, who most lack quality education?

One proposal for reorganizing American education is to offer vouchers that allow students to go to any school they wish. The idea may be unjust if it enables only the privileged, highly motivated people to migrate to better schools, leaving the poor behind, but it can favor the poor and underprivileged if the vouchers are used to connect everyone electronically to the best possible education.

In North America, such electronic education vouchers might be part of all welfare and unemployment insurance plans, designed to provide job retraining, to update education, and where necessary to provide day care for small children. Such vouchers should perhaps be provided to all people under the poverty level, and, when possible, all over the world.

This kind of foreign aid—if offered by Japan, Europe, Australia, and North America—could help the world's poor to solve their own problems (giving away information electronically would not be as expensive as other kinds of foreign aid). Indeed, this might put aid into the hands of people who most need it, without the involvement of bureaucrats and politicians. Can we propose giving foreign aid credits to individuals, including authorization to borrow a receiver plus vouchers that provide credit for on-line time and courses (often on videodisc)? And can such vouchers be tied first of all to courses that provide essential job training, entrepreneurial skills, health care, and agricultural information, and fulfill other primary needs?

The most basic and fundamental education happens, or fails to take place, at home, within the family. Electronic learning instruments at home, connected to and empowered by aspects of the worldwide electronic university, such as data bases, courseware, classes and tutoring, can also re-educate many parents as they get involved (and are guided and tutored at home) in helping their children with homework and on-line instruction. Electronic interactive education offers new possibilities for strengthening and educating the whole family.

SOFTWARE AND QUALITY

The main limits upon quality, Pelton points out, are not the technology but the *content* of education. Instead of devoting the largest share of global education funds to the communications system, the major share should henceforth go to continual teacher retraining, *and* to the development of imaginative new course software (including multimedia packages, films, and electronic textbooks).

In any case, improved quality of education, not just of technology, is what must be shared through an international educational network. More than anything else, this requires "learning teams" (a better term at this stage than teams of experts) to design educational modules that are adaptable from country to country and imaginative software that can provide what is really needed to improve the quality of instruction in every country and village. That is, instead of seeking to adapt technology created for business or other purposes, educators, including those in the Third World, should now proceed to create better software *just for learning*, the weakest link in present use of computers in education.

There can be no substitute for local teachers and counselors who can give personal attention to each learner, but we must be cautious of the notion that only the teachers need the international electronic connections, that the teachers can continue to be the experts who pass the content of education on to students. One step towards higher quality, a contribution of international electronic access, involves connecting both students and teachers to the places where the best quality exists, sometimes another school or university. The old saying, "You can lead a horse to water but you can't make him drink," is thus rephrased: "You can't make him drink but you can lead him to high-quality water that can make him thirsty."

From kindergarten to university, instructors all find it hard to leave behind the often oppressive or primitive style of education in which students face the lecturing teacher who stands or sits before the class.

Learners were expected to have such an image of the teacher on the TV screen or inside the computer in contrast to teachers and students sitting side by side as partners in learning and research, facing the world of information and learning together. Knowledge increases so fast and becomes outdated so quickly that the instructor can no longer be the expert on everything. The "electronic box" connects to the experts; the instructor then becomes colleague, friend, guide, coach, tutor, inspirer, and, alongside students, adventurer and fellow-seeker.

The global higher education network also helps everyone discover the college or neighborhood school building as a window on the world, an electronic learning center for all ages and for the entire neighborhood or community—a place for guidance, testing, tutoring, counseling, and acquiring the skills in using the electronic technology that one also uses to learn at home and at work.

ENLARGING PASSION FOR LEARNING

In 1987 George Leonard revised and reissued his book *Education and Ecstasy*, which asks why students were bored with so much of their schooling. Shouldn't they be thrilled, for example, with the exploration of the stars? Little children bring curiosity, imagination, and great excitement to learning and discovery; too often their schools rob them of all that joy in learning at an early age, so often teaching them only to cheat, to pass tests, or to escape into daydreaming or delinquency.

Instead, Leonard said, learners ought to be in a state of "ecstasy" as they explore the mystery and wonder that come with scientific discovery about the universe and the human body and brain. Leonard asks for joy and delight. Can planning for such ecstasy be on the agenda for the electronic university?

Ted Nelson is critical of those who do sloppy, half-creative work. He says that he has no interest in improving the educational system as it is. He wants to set learners on fire with enthusiasm. This inventor of hypertext and hypermedia wants to "enhance and nurture our minds and capabilities," taking us far beyond former levels of literacy to new levels of understanding and intelligence (Nelson 1987).

Linda Harasim (1990) enquires into ways that on-line education can do more than improve the learner's access to information and knowledge building, suggesting that intelligence can be enlarged and empowered to "make us better thinkers, learners and problem solvers." Joseph Pelton (1990) suggests that this should be a function of the global university as does Jerome Glenn (1989).

On the other hand, Peter and Trudy Johnson-Lenz (1989) say that hyperspace, where the electronic university exists, presents society "with enormous possibilities and equally enormous risks. It could become the new global village green where we meet to explore how to be better human beings and care for ourselves, our culture, and our planet." Peter and Trudy enthralled a large audience at a conference in Toronto in 1980, speaking on how communications technology was having a transforming effect on society. Now, after a decade of experience and creating groupware to help people work together on-line, they report that they no longer believe in such simple visions of connectivity. "Connecting people without clear purposes, processes, and norms to guide their interactions results in scattered and sporadic activity." Without planning for excellence, electronic communications are "usually unsatisfying and unfruitful."

Yet few people, they report, and especially few educators, are using hyperspace well at a time when more and more learning takes place there. What's missing is "support for different learning styles, self-directed learning, education for the whole person, and learning *how* to learn." In the future of education, as in other human systems, what happens in hyperspace and these "on-line systems are the foundation for a social architecture of the future." But, they ask, "will it become a planetary nervous system or an electronic tower of Babel?" In order to address this question they began to explore new ways of incorporating "active listening, explicit group processes and activities, emotional safety, mutual encouragement and reminders of the sacred" into on-line activities. Computer conferencing changes the participant's sense of space and time as people in different countries and time zones find new ways to meet and work together. This hyperspace is real to the world of business and finance, for example, as the place where billions of dollars leap instantly from country to country, and to the world of global politics where equally invisible and incredible events take place.

In this emerging world of hyperspace, they find, we human beings are "like astronauts experiencing zero gravity for the first time—we still have many things to learn." So Trudy and Peter invited participants to covenant together "to create a safe, supportive, and vital [on-line electronic] learning community." They agree to listen to each other with care and compassion, to speak the truth as well as they can, and to acknowledge everyone's personal wholeness and connection with the sacred. This suggests a quite different approach to global electronic education, in contrast to those who seek powerful institutional forms to guide the emerging university.

Trudy and Peter prefer to visualize self-directed on-line learners as meeting around an imaginary hearth or campfire in hyperspace. Each gathering circle shares "background information, a menu of personal self-discovery processes, and instructions," for example, on how to live with questions a few days and then return to the circle to share what has been learned. Those who plan for the electronic university must not overlook the importance of providing support for individuals using electronic group processes, "using reflection, intuition, and other forms of *inner* knowing to discover what really matters" as well as well-thought-out institutional procedures.

Educational technology becomes more sensitive and usable when it is seen as part of a living organism—not as the cold, heartless product of hardware. What is needed is not merely a humanizing of technology. Systems can be made healthy or unhealthy in large measure by our own human interaction with them. Also, humanity needs more than the ability to control the proliferation and use of technology. Higher education planners must seek ways to use it wisely and well.

"The time has come to share scarce resources . . . every university can't expect to have an expert in every field," according to a summary report (Graham 1991a). We have come to the end of an era in which colleges can be "bounded by a wall with a narrow gate" that keeps out all but a few who can afford high costs, when all students are kept "in one place at one time," sharing finite resources and faculty and when they leave, their education stops. But will the universities join to plan the new era or leave it to others?

BIBLIOGRAPHY

GENERAL BIBLIOGRAPHY

Aaron, Henry. 1990. *Setting National Priorities: Policy for the Nineties.* Washington, D.C.: The Brookings Institution.

Abrioux, Dominique. 1991. "Computer-Assisted Language Learning at a Distance: An International Survey." *American Journal of Distance Education* 5 (1): 3–14.

Alexandria Institute. 1986a. "The Library of Congress in Every Library?" *The New Alexandria* 1, no. 1 (July-August): 1–3.

———. 1986b. "What Is an Electronic Library? Characteristics of a Knowledge Resource Center." *The New Alexandria* 1, no. 1 (July-August): 1–3.

Altman, L. 1991. "Textbooks Fall Behind Advances in Medicine." *New York Times*, 7 May.

Andrews, Edmund. 1991. "Pursuing Al Sikes's Grand Agenda." *New York Times*, 2 June.

———. 1991. "Satellite Pocket Phone." *New York Times*, 15 September.

Antrim, Lance. 1986. "Computer Models as an Aid to Negotiation." Unpublished paper, Office of Technology Management, U.S. Congress.

Applegate, Alan. 1991. "N8EMR HAM Radio/Satellite BBS." *Boardwatch*, April, 33–34.

Arms, Caroline. 1989. *Campus Networking Strategies.* Bedford, Mass.: Digital Press.

———. 1990. *Campus Strategies for Libraries and Electronic Information.* Bedford, Mass.: Digital Press.

Baker, D. James. 1988. "Remote Sensing: The International Community Comes of Age." *Earthquest*, Office of Interdisciplinary Earth Studies, University Corporation for Atmospheric Research, Winter.

Baldwin, Lionel. 1984a. "An Electronic University." *IEEE Spectrum*, November.

———. 1984b. "Instructional Television." *IEEE Spectrum*, November.

———. 1991. "Higher Education Partnerships in Engineering and Science." *The Annals of the American Academy of Political and Social Science*. March, 513.

———. 1991b. Personal correspondence, February.

Barry, Yvonne. 1987. "Students Launch Space Project" (NORSTAR Norfolk Public Schools Student Team for Acoustical Research with NASA, on CompuServe computer network). *Online Today*, June.

Bates, Tony. 1991. "Review of Distance Education." *American Journal of Distance Education* 5 (1): 75–76.

Beaudoin, Michael. 1990. "The Instructor's Changing Role in Distance Education." *The American Journal of Distance Education* 4 (2): 21–29.

Becker, Joseph. 1989. "The Concept of a University of the World." *The Information Society* 6 (3): 83–92.

Begley, Sharon. 1991. "Gridlock in the Labs." *Newsweek*, 14 January.

Benne, Kenneth. 1990. *The Task of Post-Contemporary Education*. New York: Teacher's College Press.

Benveniste, Guy. 1989. *Mastering the Politics of Planning*. San Francisco: Jossey-Bass.

Berger, Knute. 1989. "The Information Ecosystem." *In Context* 23.

Block, Robert S. 1984. "A Global Information Utility." *The Futurist* 18 (12): 31–34.

Blumenstyk, Goldie. 1990. "Scholars and Libraries Ask to Get Government Data in Electronic Form." *Chronicle of Higher Education*, 28 March, A27.

Bok, Derek. 1990. *Universities and the Future of America*. Durham, N.C.: Duke University Press.

Bolter, Jay. 1991. *Writing Space*. Hillsdale, N.J.: Erlbaum.

Brand, Stewart. 1987. *The Media Lab*. New York: Viking.

Brandt, Richard. 1991. "Multimedia and Reality." *Multimedia Review* 2, no. 1 (Spring): 28–32.

Branscomb, Lewis M. 1989. "Planning the New National Network." *Educom Review* 24, no. 1 (Spring): 7–10.

Brey, Ronald, and Charles Grigsby. 1984. "A Study of Telecourse Students." *A Report from the Annenberg CPB Project*.

Brock, Dee. 1990. "Using Technology to Deliver Education." *Bulletin of the American Society for Information Science*. August-September.

Brownrigg, Edwin. 1990. "Environments for Testing and Evaluating Service and Product Innovations." *Educom Review* 25, no. 3 (Fall): 17.

Bugliarello, George. 1984. "Hyperintelligence." *The Futurist*, December.

Busby, John. 1989. "Developing a Collegewide Plan for Computer Integration." *T.H.E Journal*, special Macintosh issue.

Callihan, David. 1989. Personal correspondence with a program specialist, Volunteers in Technical Assistance.

Carlson, Patricia. 1990. "Square Books and Round." *Academic Computing* 4, no. 2 (April).

Catchpole, Michael. 1986. "A Guide to Producing and Hosting a Live-interactive Telecourse." *Distance Education* 1 (1): 129–41.

Cerf, Vinton. 1991. "Networks." *Scientific American* 265, no. 3 (September): 72–81.

Chen, Ching-chih. 1989. "The First Emperor of China's Ancient World Uncovered, from Xian to Electronic Screen." *Academic Computing* 3, no. 2 (May).

Chignell, Mark, and Richard Lacy. 1988. "Project Jefferson." *Academic Computing* 4, no. 3 (September).

Chrepta, Jay. 1988. "Creating the Planet-Wide Classroom." *Tufts Criterion*, Spring-Summer, 15.

Chute, Alan, Lee Balthazar, and Carol Poston. 1989. "Learning from Teletraining." In *Readings in Distance Learning and Instruction*, ed. Michael Moore. University Park: Pennsylvania State University.

Cisler, Steve. 1991. "Civilizing Cyberspace: Minding the Matrix." Public Access Computer Systems [on-line] Forum. L–1991, 15:35; 44, 77, 7 July.

Clark, C. G. 1989. "Speaking Personally with Armand Villarroel." *American Journal of Distance Education* 3 (2): 78–81.

Cleveland, Harlan. 1991. "Rethinking International Governance." *The Futurist*, May-June, 9–11.

Cole, George. 1991. "The Listening Box." *London Times Educational Supplement*, 8 March.

Collis, Betty A. 1991. "Telecommunications-Based Training in Europe." *The American Journal of Distance Education* 5 (2).

Commonwealth of Learning. 1990. "Quality Through Distance." *Comlearn: News Publication of the Commonwealth of Learning*, September.

Connet, Michael. 1991. "Educational-Access Cable Television." *T.H.E Journal* 19, no. 1 (August): 62–64.

Cookson, Peter. 1989. "Research on Learners..." *American Journal of Distance Education* 3 (2): 22–34.

Coombs, Norman. 1989. "Using CMC (Computer Mediated Communication) to Overcome Physical Disabilities." In *Mindweave: Communication, Computers and Distance Education*, ed. Robin Mason and Anthony Kay. New York: Pergamon.

Coons, Bill. 1989. "Providing Macintosh Access to Cornell Library's Online Catalog." *T.H.E Journal*, special Macintosh issue.

Coppola, Ralph. 1991. "SVSU Tackles Knowledge Transfer in CIESIN Project." *MichNet News*, May-June.

Cowlan, Bert. 1991. IRIDIUM Satellite Plans, on-line correspondence, 9 May.

Crane, Gregory. 1990. "Challenging the Individual: The Tradition of Hypermedia Databases." *Academic Computing* 4, no. 1 (January).

Crookall, David, and Jonathan Wickenfield. 1986. "Satellites, Computers, Politics, Languages and Gaming." *Scope*, March-April, 14–15.

Curtis, Richard. 1991. "Here Come the Cyberbooks." *Authors Guild Bulletin*, Spring-Summer, 9–13.

Davis, Watson. 1967. "The Universal Brain." In *The Growth of Knowledge*, ed. Manfred Kochen, 60–65. New York: Wiley.

Day, Carol. 1989. "Searching for Dante." *PC Computing*, May, 151–162.

DeBlasi, Mario. 1990. "World Association for the Use of Satellites in Education." Unpublished paper, Community of Mediterranean Universities, 25 June.

———. 1991. *Open and Distance Learning Newsletter*, July-August.

Deken, Joseph. 1981. *The Electronic Cottage*. New York: Bantam Books.

DeLoughry, Thomas. 1988. "Remote Instruction Using Computers Found as Effective as Classroom Sessions." *The Chronicle of Higher Education*, 20 April, A15, A21.

DeMaio, David, and Takeshi Utsumi. 1991. *User Manual of Global Lecture Hall*. Bari, Italy: Editionze Fratelli Laterza.

Dertouzos, Michael. 1991. "Communications, Computers and Networks." *Scientific American* 265, no. 3 (September): 62–69.

Dickson, David. 1988. "University Cooperation Called Key to Economic Integration of Europe." *The Chronicle of Higher Education*, 21 September.

Dille, B., and M. Mezack. 1991. "Identifying Predictors of High Risk Among Community College Telecourse Students." *American Journal of Distance Education* 5 (1): 24–35.

Ditlea, Steve. 1990. "The McDonald's of Information." *PC Computing*, October, 201–204.

Doctor, D. D. 1991. "Information Technologies and Social Equity." *Journal of the American Association for Information Science* 42, no. 3 (April): 216–28.

Domenici, Ben, and Pat Smith. 1991. "Unidata and NSFNET Keep an Eye on the Weather." *Link Letter*, January-February.

Dougherty, Richard. 1991. "Research Libraries Must Abandon the Idea that 'Bigger is Better'." *The Chronicle of Higher Education*, 19 June.

Drexler, Eric. 1987. *Engines of Creation*. New York: Doubleday.

Drucker, Peter. 1989. "Managing the Post-Business Society." *Fortune*, 3 July.

Elias, Richard. 1987. "Electronic University Expands Educational Options." *Online Today*, September.

Elkington, John, and Jonathan Shockley. 1988. *The Shrinking Planet: U.S. Information Technology and Sustainable Development*. World Resources Institute, June.

Elmore, G. C. 1991. "Planning and Developing a Multimedia Learning Environment." *T.H.E. Journal* 18, no. 7 (February): 83–88.

Eurich, Nell. 1990. *The Learning Industry: Education for Adult Workers*. Princeton: Princeton University Press.

Evans, Terry, and D. Nation, eds. 1989. *Critical Reflections on Distance Learning*. New York: Falmer Press.

Farallones Institute. "ECONET, an International, Ecological Telecommunications Network." ECONET, 15290 Coleman Valley Road, Occidental, CA 95465.

Feenberg, A., and B. Bellman. 1990. "Social Factor Research in Computer-Mediated Communications." In *Online Education: Perspectives on a New Environment*, ed. Linda Harasim. New York: Praeger.

Feigenbaum, Edward, and Pamela McCorduck. 1984. *The Fifth Generation*. New York: New American Library.

Feldman, Tony. 1989. "The Emergence of the Electronic Book." *British Library* 25.

———. 1991. "The Electronic Book." *British Book News*, February.

Fisher, Lawrence. 1990. "The Lure of Small Satellites." *New York Times*, 30 September.

Fisher, Scott. 1990. "Personal Simulations and Telepresence." *Multimedia Review* 1 (2): 24–30.

Fletcher, J. D. 1991. "Excerpts from *Effectiveness and Cost of Interactive Videodisk Instruction in Defense Training and Education*." *Multimedia Review* 2, no. 1 (Spring): 33–42.

Franklin, Jon. 1987. *Molecules of the Mind*. New York: Atheneum.

Frey, Donnalyn, and Rick Adams. 1990. *The Directory of Electronic Mail*. Sebastopol, Calif.: O'Reilly and Associates.

Friedlander, Larry. 1988. "The Shakespeare Project: Experiments in Multimedia Education." *Academic Computing* 2, no. 7 (May-June): 26–29, 66–68.

Gardner, Howard. 1983. *The Theory of Multiple Intelligences*. New York: Basic Books.

Garriott, Gary. 1990. "PACSAT Launch Boosts Third World Communications." *Vita News*, January, 4–6.

Garrison, D. R., and D. G. Shale. 1989. "Mapping the Boundaries of Distance Education: Problems in Defining the Field." In *Readings in Distance Learning and Instruction*, eds. Michael Moore and G. Christopher Clark. University Park, Pa.: American Center for the Study of Distance Education, Pennsylvania State University.

———. 1990. "The Virtual Campus: Students in an Electronic Networking Environment." Pegasus educational conference on-line in Australia.

Gast, Gerd. 1991. "Successful Online Course." Draft of paper on GLOSAS-L computer bulletin board, University of Ottawa.

Gifford, Bernard. 1991. "Cheering On Motorola University." *The Chronicle of Higher Education*, 29 January, A15.

Gilcher, Kay. 1989. "Report: A Study of Audiographic Conferencing Systems." *The American Journal of Distance Education* 3 (1): 80–82.

Gilder, George. 1990. *Life After Television*. Knoxville, Tenn.: Whittle Books.

Glenn, Jerome. 1989. *Future Mind*. Washington, D.C.: Acropolis Books.

Goodman, H.J.A. See Appendix: World Brain bibliography.

Gore, Albert. 1991. "Infrastructure for the Global Village." *Scientific American* 265, no. 3 (September): 150–53.

Graham, Ellen. 1991. "On-Line Teaching: Distance Education Uses Electronic Links to Recast the Campus." *The Wall Street Journal*, 13 September.

Greenwood, Elizabeth. 1991. "ILSs: New Emphases for the Coming Years." *T.H.E. Journal* 19, no. 2 (September): 10–14.

Gregory, David. 1988. "The Creation Station." *Academic Computing* 2, no. 1 (October): 26–27, 57–59.

Greif, Irene, ed. 1988. *Computer-Supported Cooperative Work*. Palo Alto, Calif.: Morgan Kaufman.

Griffin, Glenn, and Matthew Hodgins. 1991. "VTT in the Navy." *T.H.E Journal* 19, no. 1 (August): 65–67.

Grimes, Paul, Joyce Nielson, and James Niss. 1989. "The Performance of Non-resident Students in the 'Economics U$A' Telecourse." In *Readings in Principles of Distance Education*, eds. Michael Moore and G. Christopher Clark. University Park, Pa.: Pennsylvania State University.

Gross, Ronald. 1991. *Peak Learning.* Los Angeles: Jeremy Tarcher.

Grossbrenner, Alfred. 1985. *A Complete Handbook of Personal Computer Communications.* New York: St. Martin's Press.

Guzzardi, R. 1991. "Strategies for a Distance Education System in the Mediterranean." *Open and Distance Learning Newsletter,* July-August.

Harasim, Linda. 1990. *Online Education: Perspectives on a New Environment.* New York: Praeger.

Hart, Daniela. 1988. "Universities from European and Latin American Countries Plan Closer Ties." *The Chronicle of Higher Education,* 27 April, A43–45.

Haskins, Charles H. 1957. *The Renaissance of the 12th Century.* Cleveland: World Publishing Co.

Heinzen, T. E., and S. M. Alberico. 1990. "Using a Creativity Paradigm to Evaluate Teleconferencing." *American Journal of Distance Education* 4(3): 3–12.

Heller, Nelson. 1990. "DESKlab Unveiled for Underprepared Students." *The Heller Report* 1, no. 7 (July).

———. 1991a. "EDSAT Study Formally Proposes Education Satellite." *The Heller Report* 2, no. 6 (March): 8–9.

———. 1991b. "W. Va. College is Launch Site for NASA Classroom of the Future." *The Heller Report* 2, no. 6 (March): 9–10.

———. 1991c. "Cluster by Cluster Kansas Brings Two-Way Video to Classrooms." *The Heller Report* 2, no. 7 (April): 2–3.

———. 1991d. "The Second Boom." *The Heller Report* 2, no. 8 (May): 9.

———. 1991e. "Norpack Seeks Connection . . ." *The Heller Report* 2, no. 11 (July).

———. 1991f. "New Videodisk System." *The Heller Report* 2, no. 11 (July).

———. 1991g. "Discovery Interactive Library Unveiled." *The Heller Report* 2, no. 11 (July).

———. 1991h. "New Videodisc System Lets Teachers Make Customized Videotapes." *The Heller Report* 2, no. 11 (July).

———. 1991i. "NTU Projects Revenues." *The Heller Report* 2, no. 6 (February).

Hezel, Richard. 1990. *Statewide Planning for Telecommunication in Education.* Annenberg CPB Project. Syracuse, N.Y.: Hezel Associates.

———. 1991. "Annenberg Gives Back $60 Million." *Strata Gems* 2(1): 2.

Hiltz, Starr Roxanne. 1988a. "A Virtual Classroom on EIES, a Final Evaluation Report." Unpublished, New Jersey Institute of Technology.

———. 1988b. "Computer Mediated Communications and Developing Countries." *Telematics* 5(4): 357–76.

———. 1990. "Evaluating the Virtual Classroom." In *Online Education: Perspectives on a New Environment,* ed. Linda Harasim. New York: Praeger.

Hudson, Heather, and Meheroo Jussawalla. 1987. "Satellite Communications and Development." In *Satellites International,* eds. Joseph Pelton and John Howkins. London: Macmillan.

Hughes, David. 1991a. "In the Beginning Was the Word." *Netweaver* 7 (Winter).

———. 1991b. Personal phone call, 5 April.

———. 1991c. "Now is Not the Time to Write the Law on Freedom of Electronic Speech." *Research and Education Networking* 2, no. 4 (May): 6–7.

IBM. 1990. "Networks: The Beginning of an Intellectual Revolution." International Business Machines Corp.

INTELSAT. 1991a. "INTELSAT Board of Governors Concludes 88th Meeting: Acts on Upcoming Launch and Boost Missions," 13 March.

———. 1991b. "INTELSAT Global Traffic Meeting Sets Record Attendance." 8 May.

Ishi, Hiroshi. 1990. "Computer Supported Cooperative Work." *Whole Earth*, no. 69 (Winter): 48–50.

Itzkan, Seth. 1987. "The Japanese Tele-connection." *Impact*. The Boston Computer Society, Spring.

———. n.d. "The Emergence of the Global Classroom." Somerville, Mass.: privately published report on joint USA-Japan project.

Jaeger, George. 1990a. "Brief Assessment of Online Freshman Comp Class." Distance Learning Forum on ISAAC computer bulletin board, Spring.

———. 1990b. "Cerritos College, a California Community College, Offers Online Courses." *The Online Journal of Distance Education* 4(2).

Jason Foundation. 1989. "Underwater Exploration via Telepresence: An Educational Adventure Through Worldwide Communications Technology." Herndon, Va.: The Jason Project.

Johansen, Robert. 1988. *Groupware: Computer Support for Business Teams*. New York: Free Press.

Johnson-Lenz, Peter and Trudy. 1981. "Consider the Groupware." In *Studies of Computer-Mediated Communication Systems*. Research Report #16, Computerized Conferencing and Communications Center, New Jersey Institute of Technology.

———. 1989. "Humanizing Hyperspace." *In Context* 23.

Jones, C., and W. M. Timpson. 1991. "Technologically Mediated Staff Development." *American Journal for Distance Education* 5(1): 51–56.

Jones, Richard. 1989. "Online Catalog Research in Europe." *Journal of the American Society for Information Science* 40, no. 3 (May): 153–57.

Jussawalla, M., T. Okuma, and T. Araki. 1989. *Information Technology and Global Interdependence*. Westport, Conn.: Greenwood.

Karraker, Robert. 1991. "Highways of the Mind." *Whole Earth*, no. 70 (Spring): 4–11.

Kay, Alan. 1991. "Computers, Networks and Education." *Scientific American* 265, no. 3 (September): 138–48.

Kearsley, Greg. 1985. *Training for Tomorrow*. Reading, Mass.: Addison-Wesley.

———. 1987. *Artificial Intelligence and Instruction*. Reading, Mass.: Addison-Wesley.

Keegan, Desmond. 1989. *The Foundations of Distance Education*. New York: St. Martin's Press.

Keith, Harry. 1991. "Distance Education: A Survey of Current Literature." *British Book News*, April.

Kerr, Elaine, and Starr Roxanne Hiltz. 1982. *Computer Mediated Communication Systems: Status and Evaluation*. New York: Academic Press.

———. 1990. Review of *Online Education: Perspectives on a New Environment*, edited by Linda Harasim. *The American Journal of Distance Education* 4(3): 73–74.

Kerwin, William. 1989. "Academic Computing." *Educom Review* 24, no. 1 (Spring): 35–37.

Kibbey, Mark, and Nancy Evans. 1989. "The Network is the Library." *Educom Review* 24, no. 3 (Fall): 15–20.

Killman, Ralph. 1989. "Tomorrow's Company Won't Have Walls." *New York Times*, 18 June.

Kingsbury, David. 1990. "Computational Science." *Edu Magazine*, issue 53 (Spring): 7–9.

Kirby, Richard, and Parker Rossman. 1990. *Christians and the World of Computers: Professional and Social Excellence*. Philadelphia: Trinity Press International.

Kochen, Manfred. 1988. "Extending the Human Record." Report to the Automatic Systems Office. Washington, D.C.: Library of Congress.

Koenenn, Connie. 1989. "Changing Book Formats." *Los Angeles Times*, 28 February.

Koul, B. N., and J. Jenkins. *Distance Education*. London: Kogan Page.

Kramer, Krista, et al. 1989. "Computers and Students with Disabilities." Project EASI (Easy Access to Software for Instruction). *Educom Review*, Fall.

Krueger, Anne, and Vernon Ruttan. 1989. *Aid and Development*. Baltimore: Johns Hopkins University Press.

Krueger, Myron. 1983 (updated 1991). *Artificial Reality*. Reading, Mass.: Addison-Wesley.

———. 1990. "Reflections on the World of Multimedia Computing." *Multimedia Review* 1, no. 2 (Summer): 21–34.

Lauby, Paul. 1987. "The New Challenge to Higher Education in Asia." *Breakthrough*, Spring/Summer.

Laurel, Brenda. 1989. *The Art of Human-Computer Interface Design*. Reading, Mass.: Addison-Wesley.

———. 1990. "Visual Reality Design." *Multimedia Review*. 1, no. 2 (Summer): 14–17.

Leibbrandt, G. J. 1989. "An Open University in the SADCC Region (Angola to Zambia)." Unpublished paper prepared for the Commission of the European Communities, The Hague, Netherlands.

Leonard, George. 1987. *Education and Ecstasy*. Berkeley: North Atlantic Press.

Levinson, Paul. 1988. "TRANSCRIPT: Popular Culture and the Media." ConnectEd Program in Media Studies, online course, April-May. New York: New School.

———. 1989. "Intelligent Writing: The Electronic Liberation of Text." Paper presented at Annual Meeting of the American Academy for the Advancement of Science, San Francisco, 16 January.

———. 1990. "Computer Conferencing in the Context of the Evolution of Media." In *Online Education: Perspectives on a New Environment*, ed. Linda Harasim. New York: Praeger.

———. 1991. Personal telephone conversation, 29 May.

Lewis, Peter. 1991. "The Electronic Edge." *New York Times* educational supplement, 7 April.

Litvak, Jorge. 1986. "Micros Speed Medical Information Between Chile and the U.S.A." *International Informatics Access* 1, no. 3 (November-December): 3–7.

LNC Design Project. 1989. "The Learning Network Corporation." SYNCOM, 249 Oxford Road, Illovo, South Africa.

London, Herbert L. 1987. "The Death of the University." *The Futurist* 21 (May-June): 17–22.

Love, Sharon, et al. 1991. "Design Techniques for Ensuring Structure and Flexibility in a Hypermedia Environment." *Multimedia Review* 2, no. 2 (Summer): 34–43.

Lucier, Richard. 1990. "Knowledge Management: Refining Roles in Scientific Communication." *Educom Review* 25, no. 3 (Fall): 21–29.

Lundin, Roy. 1988. "Communication and Information Technologies in Business and Education." Brisbane, Australia: College of Advanced Education.

Lunin, Lois. 1988. "Optical Memory Cards." *Bulletin of the American Society for Information Science*, April-May, 35–36.

———. 1989. "Perspectives on Hypertext." *Journal of the American Society for Information Science* 40, no. 3 (May): 159–63.

Lynch, Clifford. 1990. Review of *The Linked Systems Project: A Networking Tool for Libraries*, edited by Judith Fenley and Beecher Williams. *Journal of the American Society for Information Science* 41(4): 305–6.

Mabus, Ray. 1991. "A New Light in Education." *T.H.E. Journal* 19, no. 1 (August): 53–56.

Mageau, Therese. 1991. "Ten Smart Lessons for the 90's." *Agenda* 1, no. 1 (Spring): 48–51.

Marien, Michael, ed. 1991. *Future Survey Annual*. Bethesda, Md.: World Future Society.

Markoff, John. 1989a. "The Big News in Tiny Computers." *New York Times*, 14 May.

———. 1989b. "Scientists Share Data at Speed of Light." *New York Times*, 4 June.

———. 1991. "Locking the Doors of the Electronic Global Village." *New York Times*, 26 July.

Marraccini, Jeff. 1991. "Bulletin Boards on the Internet." *MichNet News*, March.

Mason, Robin, and Anthony Kaye. 1989. *Mindweave: Communication, Computers and Distance Education*. New York: Pergamon.

———. 1990. "Toward a New Paradigm for Distance Education." In *Online Education: Perspectives on a New Environment*, ed. Linda Harasim. New York: Praeger.

McDonald. 1991. "Despite Benefits, Electronic Journals Will Not Replace Print." *The Chronicle of Higher Education*, 27 February.

McGregor, Pat. 1991. "FredMail Network." *MichNet News* 6(2): 6–7.

Meeks, Brock. 1987. "The Quiet Revolution: On-line Education Becomes a Real Alternative." *Byte*, February, 183–84.

Merriam, Sharon, and Phyllis Cunningham. 1989. *Handbook of Adult and Continuing Education*. San Francisco: Jossey-Bass.

Meuter, Ralph, and Leslie Wright. 1989. "Telecommunications: CSU Chico." *T.H.E Journal* 16, no. 9 (May): 70–73.

Mooney, Carolyn. 1988. "New Data Base Will Inform Companies About Professors' Research Specialities." *Chronicle of Higher Education*, 16 November, A13.

Moore, Michael. 1990. *Contemporary Issues in Distance Education*. Riverside, N.J.: Pergamon Press.

Moore, Michael, and G. Christopher Clark. 1989a. *Readings in Principles of Distance*

Education. University Park, Pa.: American Center for the Study of Distance Education, Pennsylvania State University.

———. 1989b. *Readings in Distance Learning and Instruction*, no. 2. University Park: Pennsylvania State University.

Muckridge, Ian, and David Kaufman. 1986. *Distance Education in Canada*. Buckenham, Kent: Croom Helm.

Murgatroyd, S., and A. Woudstra. 1989. "Issues in the Management of Distance Education." *American Journal of Distance Education* 3(1): 4–19.

Murray, Carolyn, and Ethel Auster. 1990. "High Tech Flight Training." In *Proceedings of the 53rd ASIS Annual Meeting*, ed. Diane Henderson. Medford, N.J.: Learned Information, Inc.

Naisbitt, John, and Patricia Aburdene. 1990. *Megatrends 2000*. New York: William Morrow.

Negroponte, Nicholas. 1991. "Products and Services for Computer Networks." *Scientific American* 265, no. 3 (September): 106–113.

Nelson, Ted. 1987. *Computer Lib/Dream Machines*. Brookline, Mass.: Microsoft Press.

Nevins, C. L., and C. Urbanowicz. 1991. "Extra-Terrestrial Education: Not Science Fiction at All!" Paper presented at the American Association for the Advancement of Science, Washington, D.C., 14–19 February.

Newman, Denis. 1990. "Cognitive and Technical Issues in the Design of Educational Computer Networking." In *Online Education: Perspectives on a New Environment*, ed. Linda Harasim. New York: Praeger.

Newroe, Kathleen. 1988. "Distance Learning." *Whole Earth*, no. 64, Winter.

NeXT on Campus. 1991. "Fluxbase: Cataloging and Experiencing Non-traditional Art with Technology," "Mathematic Lab," and "Drawing Students into Research." Spring, 10–18.

Nickerson, R. S. 1989. *Technology in Education*. Hillsdale, N.J.: Erlbaum Associates.

Omnet. 1988. "Forty-One and Still Counting." *ScienceNet News*, May.

Opper, Susanna. 1988. "A Groupware Toolbox." *Byte*, December, 275.

The Orbiter. 1990. "Society of Satellite Professionals Videoconference . . ." November-December.

Papert, Seymour. 1980. *Mind Storms*. New York: Basic Books.

Parker, Lorne. 1991. "Evaluations." *Satellite Learning* 2, no. 1 (Spring): 25.

Parnell, Dale. 1990. *Dateline 2000: The New Higher Education Agenda*. Washington, D.C.: The Community College Press.

Paulsen, Morten. 1987/88. "In Search of a Virtual School." *T.H.E Journal*, December-January, 71–76.

———. 1991a. "The ICDL Database for Distance Education." *DEOSNEWS* (on-line newsletter). American Center for Distance Education, May.

———. 1991b. "The ICDL Database for Distance Education." *The American Journal of Distance Education* 5(2).

PBS Education Services. 1989. "Introducing the PBS Education Pipeline," "PBS Adult Learning Satellite Service," and "Introducing the Business Channel," PBS Adult Learning Services.

Pelton, Joseph. 1990a. *FutureTalk*. Boulder, Colo.: Cross Communications.

————. 1990b. "Technology and Education." Paper presented at the International Distance Education Conference, Caracas, Venezuela, November.

————. 1991. "The Future of Tele-Education." Paper presented at National University Teleconference Network conference, Orlando, Florida, February.

Pelton, Joseph, and John Howkins. 1987. *Satellites International*. London: Macmillan.

Perot, Ross. 1989. "Educating Our Children." *Educom Review* 24, no. 1 (Spring): 14–17.

Pierce, Richard. 1990. "Information Technology and the Humanities." *Bulletin of the American Society for Information Science* 16, no. 3 (February-March).

Por, George. 1987. "Multimedia Teleconferencing Symposium." *Netweaver* (on-line electronic journal) 2(10).

Pugliatti, Enzo. 1989. "Low-Cost Networking Experiences in Latin America." Paper presented at Latin American Networking Workshop, San Jose, Costa Rica, 14–16 June.

Quarterman, John. 1990. *The Matrix*. Bedford, Mass.: Digital Press.

————. 1991. "The Maturation of the Matrix." *Netweaver* (on-line electronic journal) 7 (Winter).

Rasmussen, T., J. Bang, and K. Lunby. 1991. "When Academia Goes Online." *DEOS Online Newsletter* 1(4).

Reitman, Valerie. 1991. "Video Store May Go the Way of the Edsel." Knight-Ridder Newspapers, 24 February.

Rheingold, Howard. 1986. "Virtual Communities." *Whole Earth Review*, Summer.

Richards, David. 1990. "The Research Libraries Group." In *Campus Strategies for Libraries and Electronic Information*, ed. Caroline Arms. Bedford, Mass.: Digital Press.

Rickard, Jack. 1991a. "More on Getting Access to Internet." *Boardwatch* 5, no. 4 (May): 28–32.

————. 1991b. "K12Net—Linking Bulletin Boards for Education." *Boardwatch* 5, no. 6 (June): 39–40.

————. 1991c. "Iridium Satellite Project Update." *Boardwatch* (November): 10.

Ritchie, H., and T. J. Newby. 1989. "Classroom Lecture/Discussion vs. Live Television Instruction." *American Journal of Distance Education* 3(3): 36–45.

Rossman, Parker. 1982. "The Coming Great Electronic Encyclopedia." *The Futurist* 26, no. 4 (August): 53–57.

————. 1985. *Computers: Bridges to the Future*. Valley Forge, Pa.: Judson Press.

Rothman, D. H. 1990. *The Complete Laptop Computer Guide*. New York: St. Martin's Press.

Ryland, Jane. 1990. "Higher Education: Coming Around to Competitive Systems." *Edu Magazine*, issue 53 (Summer): 19–23.

Sanders, Kevin. 1986. "Etiquette for the Age of Transparency: Public Access to Public Monitoring from Space." *Whole Earth Review* 50 (Spring).

Schiller, H. I. 1989. *Culture, Inc.: The Corporate Takeover of Public Expression*. New York: Oxford.

Schmidt, H. 1989. "New Methods Fuel Effort to Decode Human Genes." *New York Times*, 9 May.

Schmitt, Marilyn. 1990. "Scholars Must Take the Lead in Computerization in the Humanities." *The Chronicle of Higher Education*, 21 November.

Sculley, John. 1988. *Odyssey*. New York: Harper and Row.

Shamonsky, Dorothy. 1991. "Rancho Deluxe." *Multimedia Review* 2, no. 2 (Summer): 3–8.

Shane, Harold G. 1989. "Britain's University of the Air." *The Futurist*, July-August.

Sharma, Motilal. 1986. *Issues in Distance Education*. Resource Paper, Regional Seminar on Distance Education, 25 November–3 December, Bangkok, Thailand.

Singhal, Arvind, and E. M. Rogers. 1989. *India's Information Revolution*. Newbury Park, Calif.: Sage Publications.

Smart Card. 1991. "The Smart Card Explosion in France." *French Advances in Science and Technology*, Spring.

Smith, Eleanor. 1987. "Windows on the Mind." *Omni* 10, no. 9 (May).

Smith, Page. 1990. *Killing the Spirit: Higher Education in America*. New York: Viking.

Smith, Pat. 1991. "Networking 'Down Under' (Australia) with AARNet." *Link Letter*, January-February, 3, 6.

Spender, Barry, and Dennis Schall. 1990. "The Yugtarvik Museum Project Using Interactive Multimedia for Cross-Cultural Distance Education." *Academic Computing* 3, no. 3 (April).

Spier, Andre. 1991. Personal correspondence, 15 May.

Spring, Michael. 1990. "Informating with Virtual Reality." *Multimedia Review* 1, no. 2 (Summer): 5–13.

Sproull, Lee, and Sara Kiesler. 1991. "Computers, Networks and Work." *Scientific American* 265, no. 3 (September): 116–123.

Stefik, Mark, and John Seely Brown. 1989. "Toward Portable Ideas." In *Technological Support for Work Group Collaboration*, ed. Marrethe Olson. Hillsdale, N.J.: Lawrence Erlbaum Associates.

Steward, John. 1991. Personal correspondence from headquarters of the Commonwealth of Learning, 25 June.

Stewart, Doug. 1991. "Artificial Reality." *Smithsonian*, no. 10 (January): 36–45.

Stuart, Rory, and John Thomas. 1991. "The Implications of Education in Hyperspace." *Multimedia Review* 2, no. 2 (Summer): 17–27.

Sutton, Francis. 1990. *A World to Make*. New Brunswick, N.J.: Transaction Publishers.

Taub, Jack. 1990. "The Education Utility." Paper presented at the University of the World Annual Meeting, Atlanta, Georgia, 14 October.

Tessler, Lawrence. 1991. "Networked Computing in the 1990's." *Scientific American* 265, no. 3 (September): 86–93.

Thorkildsen, Ron, and Susan Friedman. 1984. "Videodisks in the Classroom." *T.H.E Journal* 11, no. 4 (April).

Thurber, B. D., et al. 1991. "The Book, the Computer and the Humanities." *T.H.E Journal* 19, no. 1 (August): 57–61.

Traub, David. 1990. "A View from Route 128: Simulated World as Classroom, the Potential for Designed Learning within Virtual Environments." *Multimedia Review* 1, no. 2 (Summer): 18–23.

Trujillo, Ivan. 1988. "Academic Computing: The Los Andes Strategy." *EDUCOM Review* 24, no. 2 (Summer): 32–38.

Turner, Judith. 1988a. "Project Linking Different Computers May Alter the Way Scholars Collaborate." *Chronicle of Higher Education*, 16 March, A20.

———. 1988b. "Plan for $5 Million Prototype." *Chronicle of Higher Education*, 1 June.

———. 1990a. "Librarians Rank Their Preferences of On-Line Information." *Chronicle of Higher Education*, 14 November.

———. 1990b. "U. of Southern California Revamps Computer Network to Offer Broad Access to Information." *The Chronicle of Higher Education*, 28 November, A19.

Turner, Sandra. 1989. "Linking Land-Surface and Atmospheric General Circulation Models." *Global Change Newsletter*, Office of Interdisciplinary Earth Studies, University Corporation for Atmospheric Research, 2.

———. 1990. "Enormous Changes in Scholarly Publishing." *The Chronicle of Higher Education*, 21 November.

Turoff, Murray. 1982. "On the Design of an Electronic University." Papers in ConnectEd Online Library.

Turoff, Murray, and S. R. Hiltz. 1988. "Computer Mediated Communications and Developing Countries." *Telematics and Informatics* 5(4): 357–76.

TWICS (Two Way Information Communication System). 1988. "DASnet: Intersystem E-mail Exchange." Tokyo: International Education Center.

Underwood, Kenneth. 1969. *The Church, the University, and Social Policy*. Vol. 2, *Working and Technical Papers for the Danforth Study*. Middletown, Conn.: Wesleyan University Press.

Urbanowicz, C. F. 1989. "Satellites, the Global Village, and Tele-Education." In *Space 30*, ed. Joseph Pelton. Alexandria, Va.: Society of Satellite Professionals.

Utsumi, Takeshi. 1989. "A Vision That Can Change the World: [report on] Pacific Basin Telecast for Global Education." Paper presented at the First Annual Meeting of the University of the World, University of Michigan, 14–16 October.

———. 1990. "Global Education for Fostering Global Citizenship." *Transnational Perspectives* (Geneva, Switzerland) 15(2): 23–36.

Utsumi, T., P. Mikes, and P. Rossman. 1986. "Peace Gaming with Open Modeling Network." In *Computer Networks and Simulation II*, ed. S. Schoemaker. Amsterdam: North Holland.

Utsumi, Takeshi, and Gerald Mische. 1989. "Proposal of Space Satellite Library System." Global Education Associates, unpublished paper, 18 February.

Utsumi, Takeshi, Parker Rossman, and Steven Rosen. 1988. "The Global Electronic University." *American Journal of Distance Education* 2(2): 57–67.

———. 1989. "Global Education for the 21st Century." *T.H.E Journal* 16, no. 7 (March): 75–77.

UW. 1991. *The University of the World Newsletter*, April.

Vagianos, Louis. 1988. "The Third World Perspective." *Bulletin of the American Association for Information Science* 14, no. 3 (February-March): 23–26.

Van Camp, Rosemary. 1988. "The Presidents' Conference." *Tufts Criterion*, Fall 18–19.

Van Houweling, Douglas. 1989. "The National Network." *Educom Review* 24, no. 2 (Summer): 14–18.

Volunteers in Technical Assistance. 1987. *Packet Radio: Communications Technology*. Annual report.

Von Hasselt, Kelvin. 1990. "International Student Editions." *British Book News*, July.

Wagner, E. D. 1990. "Looking at Distance Education through Technological Eyes." *American Journal of Distance Education* 4(1): 53–69.

Walser, Randal. 1990a. "Elements of a Cyberspace Playhouse." *Multimedia Review* 1, no. 2 (Summer): 35–42.

———. 1990b. "The Emerging Technology of Cyberspace." *Multimedia Review* 1, no. 2 (Summer): 35–42.

Washor, Elliot, and Deborah Couture. 1990. "A Distance Learning System that Pays All Its Own Costs." *T.H.E Journal* 17, no. 12 (December): 62–63.

Watkins, Beverly. 1991. "New Group to Promote Internet's Role in Global Computer Networking." *Wall Street Journal*, 11 September.

Weinstein, S. B., and P. W. Shumate. 1989. "Beyond the Telephone." *The Futurist*, November-December, 8–12.

Weiser, Mark. 1991. "The Computer for the 21st Century." *Scientific American* 265, no. 3 (September): 94–104.

Wells, H. G. 1938. *World Brain*. Garden City, N.J.: Doubleday Doran.

Weyh, John, and Joseph Crook. 1988. "CAI Drill and Practice: Is It Really Bad?" *Academic Computing* 2, no. 7 (May-June): 32–36, 52–54.

WFS. 1991. "Australia's City of the Future." *The Futurist*, January-February. For more information, writer Counselor for Industry and Science, Embassy of Australia, 1601 Mass. Ave. NW, Washington, D.C. 20036.

Wilder, Clinton. 1990. "An Electronic Classroom." *Computerworld*, 26 February.

Wilkes, C. W. and B. R. Burnham. 1991. "Adult Learner Motivations and Electronic Distance Education." *American Journal of Distance Education* 5(1): 43–50.

Wilshire, Bruce. 1990. *The Moral Collapse of the University*. Albany: State University of New York Press.

Wilson, David. 1991. "Testing Time for Electronic Journals." *The Chronicle of Higher Education*, 11 September, A22.

Wojciechowski, Jerry. 1986. "Computing Systems in an Ecology of Knowledge." *Future Computing Systems* (Oxford University Press) 1(4): 334–52.

Wood, R. C. 1989. "Lost in the Translation." *P.C. Computing*, August.

Wright, Gregory, and Stan Pokras. 1990. "Linking the World's Idea-Gathering Organizations to Create an Electronic/Print 'Global Suggestion Box'." Available from 14161 Riverside Drive, #3, Sherman Oaks, CA 91423.

Wright, Karen. 1990. "The Road to the Global Village." *Scientific American* 264, no. 3 (March).

Wulf, William, and Laurence Rosenberg. 1990. "Towards a National Collaboratory." *Edu Magazine*, issue 53 (Spring): 2–4.

Yager, Tom. 1991. "Computers Go Video with NEC's PC-VCR." *Byte* 16, no. 9 (September): 307–9.

Yarrish, Edward. 1991. "The Fully Electronic University." Paper presented at Applications of Computer Conferencing Conference, Ohio State University, 13–15 June.

Young, Luke T., et al. 1988. "Academic Computing in the Year 2000." *Academic Computing* 2, no. 7 (May-June): 8–12, 62–65.

WORLD BRAIN BIBLIOGRAPHY

Andel, J. 1987. "Report on World Brain Session." ASIS World Brain Group, unpublished paper.
———. 1991. "Knowledge is Power..." *The Express* (Allentown, Pa.), 6 September.
Arms, Caroline. 1990. *Campus Strategies for Libraries and Electronic Information.* Bedford, Mass.: Digital Press.
Block, Robert S. 1984. "A Global Information Utility." *The Futurist*, December.
Bohnert, H. G., and Manfred Kochen. 1963. "The Automated Multi-Level Encyclopedia as a New Mode of Scientific Communication." In *Automation and Scientific Communication*, vol. 2. Washington, D.C.: American Documentation Institute.
Brand, Stewart. 1987. *The Media Lab: Inventing the Future at MIT.* New York: Viking Press.
Breton, Ernest J. 1988. "Creating a Corporate Brain." *Bulletin of the American Society for Information Science*, October-November.
Bugliarello, George. 1984. "Hyperintelligence." *The Futurist*, December.
Bush, Vannevar. 1945. "As We May Think." *Atlantic Monthly* 176(1).
———. 1967. "MEMEX Revisited." *Science Is Not Enough.* New York: William Morrow.
Clarke, Arthur C. 1962. *Profiles of the Future.* New York: Harper and Row.
Collison, Robert. 1966. *Encyclopedias: Their History Throughout the Ages.* New York: Hafner Publishing.
Comenius, John Amos (Komensky). 1657. *Didacta Magna (The Great Didactic).* Trans. and ed. M. W. Keating. London: Adam and Charles Black, 1907. (It is reported that Comenius developed the idea even more in *Pansophic Prodromus*, c.1640.)
Davis, Watson. 1967. "The Universal Brain." In *The Growth of Knowledge*, ed. Manfred Kochen, 60–65. New York: Wiley.
DeSolla Price, Derek. 1979. "Knowledge Space in Compact Storage and Some Distinctions Regarding a World Mind, a World Encyclopedia, and a World Data Bank." Paper presented at the World Mind Group Colloquium, Banff, Alberta, 16 May. Recorded on sound cassette, available from H.J.A. Goodman, University of Calgary, Calgary, Alta., Canada, T2N 1N4.
Deutsch, Karl W. 1950. "Higher Education and the Unity of Knowledge." In *Goals for American Education*, eds. Lyman Bryson, L. Finklestein, and R. M. MacIver. New York: Harper and Row.
Garfield, Eugene. 1968. "World Brain or Memex? Mechanical and Intellectual Requirements for Universal Bibliographic Control." In *The Foundations of Access to Knowledge*, ed. E. B. Montgomery. Syracuse, N.Y.: Syracuse University Press.
———. 1975. "The World Brain as Seen by an Information Entrepreneur." In *Information for Action: From Knowledge to Wisdom*, ed. Manfred Kochen. New York: Academic Press.

———. 1977. "Towards the World Brain." In *Essays of an Information Scientist*, ed. E. Garfield. Philadelphia: ISI Press.

Glushko, Robert J. 1990. "Designing a Hypertext Electronic Encyclopedia." *ASIS Bulletin* 16, no. 3 (February-March): 14–16, 21, 22.

Goodman, H.J.A. 1972. "The Establishment of UNISIST—the World Science Information Network—as a Step Toward the World Brain." In *Proceedings of the 35th Annual Supplement Meeting*, ed. John H. Wilson. Washington, D.C.: American Society for Information Science.

———. 1974. "REGISTER ᴵᴵᴵ, Research and Educational Ganglion and International Synergistic Trecupal Encyclopedic Registry and Repository." Unpublished paper.

———. 1977. "Planning and Plans for National Library and Information Services." In *Encyclopedia of Library and Information Science*, eds. Allen Kent et al., vol. 22, 338–41. New York: Dekker.

———. 1983. "The Development of National and International Information Systems and Networks . . ." In *Information Science in Action—System Design: Proceedings of the NATO Study Institute on Information Science*, eds. Anthony Debons and A. G. Larson, 338–41. Boston: Sijthoff and Noordhoff International Publishers.

———. 1987. "The World Brain/World Encyclopedia Concept: Its Historical Roots and the Contribution of H.J.A. Goodman to the Ongoing Evolution and Implementation of the Concept." In *Proceedings of the 50th Annual Meeting of the American Association for Information Science*, ed. Ching-chih Chen, vol. 24, 91–98.

Goodman, H.J.A., and Anthony Debons. 1991. "The Senior Scholars 'State of the Art' Cumulative Online Continuously Updated Statement (SAS) System/Network." Unpublished proposal to University of the World-EDUCOM-ASIS World Brain Group.

Gordon, Michael, David Blair, and Robert Lindsay. 1989. "In Memoriam: Manfred Kochen 1928–1989." *Journal of the American Society for Information Science* 40(4): 223–25.

Gull, C. D. 1987. "Historical Note: Information Science and Technology: From Coordinate Indexing to the Global Brain." *Journal of the American Society for Information Science*, no. 5 (September): 338–366.

Harmon, Glynn. 1973. *Human Memory and Knowledge*. Westport, Conn.: Greenwood Press.

———. 1988. "Toward Encyclopedic Intelligence." *ASIS Bulletin*, October-November, 24–27.

Hilton, Howard. 1967. "A Code for the Unique Identification of Recorded Knowledge and Information." Springfield, Ohio: Clearing House for Federal Scientific and Technical Information.

Kochen, Manfred. 1967. *The Growth of Knowledge*. New York: Wiley.

———. 1972. "WISE, a World Information Synthesis and Encyclopedia." *Journal of Documentation* 28:4.

———., ed. 1975. *Information for Action: From Knowledge to Wisdom*. New York: Academic Press.

———. 1987. "A Conversation with Dr. Manfred Kochen." Recorded at the Pioneers Luncheon, ASIS 1987, in Boston, Mass., 6 October. (Audio tapes of 1987 and 1988 ASIS World Brain sessions can be obtained from Minute Tapes International, Sunnyvale, Calif.)

——. 1988. "Extending the Human Record." Report to the Library of Congress, Washington, D.C., Automated Systems Office.

Kolata, Gina. 1991. "Brains at Work." *New York Times Special Section on Education*, 6 January.

Lucier, Richard. 1990. "Knowledge Management: Refining Roles in Scientific Communication." *Educom Review*, Fall.

Nelson, Ted. 1987. *Computer Lib/Dream Machines*. Brookline, Mass.: Microsoft Press.

Pagels, H. R. 1988. *The Dreams of Reason*. New York: Simon and Schuster.

Pelton, Joseph. 1989. "Telepower: The Emerging Global Brain." *The Futurist*, September-October.

Rayward, W. B. 1975. *The Universe of Information: The Work of Paul Otlet for Documentation and International Organization*. The Hague, Holland: FID.

Rossman, Parker. 1982. "The Coming Great Electronic Encyclopedia." *The Futurist*, August.

Rossman, Parker, and R. Kirby. 1990. *Christians and the World of Computers: Professional and Social Excellence*. London: SCM Press.

Schmitt, Marilyn. 1990. "Scholars Must Take the Lead in Computerization in the Humanities." *The Chronicle of Higher Education*, 21 November.

Scullion, Joseph F. 1987. "Overview of CYC Project at MCC." AFIT AOG/AAAIC Joint Conference, Dayton, Ohio, Microelectronics and Computer Technology Corporation.

Teilhard de Chardin, Pierre. 1964. *The Future of Man*. New York: Harper and Row.

——. 1969. *The Phenomenon of Man*. New York: Harper and Row.

Turoff, Murray. 1977. "An Online Intellectual Community or MEMEX Revisited." Paper presented at annual meeting of the American Association for the Advancement of Science, Denver, Colo.

Vladutz, George. 1984. "The World Brain Today: Scientographic Databases" in *Database Management*, ed. Herbert Solomon, 215 ff. Stanford, Calif.: Stanford University Press.

——. 1987. "The World Brain Today: The Scientographic Approach to Knowledge Representation." Paper presented at Midwifing the World Brain session, American Association for Information Science meeting, 6 October.

Wells, H. G. 1938. *World Brain*. Garden City, N.J.: Doubleday Doran.

——. 1942. "Science and the World Mind." Lecture delivered at the Royal Institution, 7 September 1941. London: New Europe Publishing Co.

Wright, Gregory, and Stan Pokras. 1990. "Linking the World's Idea-Gathering Organizations to Create an Electronic/Print 'Global Suggestion Box'." Available from 14161 Riverside Drive, #3, Sherman Oaks, CA 91423.

Appendix: Resource List

Any teacher, student, administrator, or interested citizen who would like to learn how to participate in planning for global higher education can pay a fee to and receive publications from:

- The University of the World, #205, 1055 Torrey Pines Blvd., LaJolla, CA 92037.
- GLOSAS/Global University project, 43–23 Colden St., Flushing, NY 11355 (has a handbook on technology and methods for experimenting with a global classroom and also has an on-line journal on several computer networks).
- American Center for the Study of Distance Education, College of Education, Rackley Building, The Pennsylvania State University, University Park, PA 16802 (also has an on-line journal).
- Global Education Associates, #570, 475 Riverside Drive, New York, NY 10015.

The main point of this book has been to show that enough is now happening in global electronic higher education to justify a more comprehensive book than this collection of experiments, proposals, and other ideas. If you send me your ideas, I will pass them on to the long-range planning and dreaming committees whose work will be at the heart of a more adequate book.

Parker Rossman
3 Lemmon Dr.
Columbia, MO 65201

INDEX

About the Author

PARKER ROSSMAN is Vice-President of the Global Systems Analysis and Simulation Project (GLOSAS/USA) and Chair of the GLOSAS/Global University-Long-Range Planning Committee. The former Dean of the Ecumenical Education Center at Yale University, he has published several books and more than a hundred articles on computers and education.

DATE DUE

DEMCO 38-296